A PRICE ABOVE RUBIES

A PRICE ABOVE RUBIES
Boaz Yakin

faber and faber

First published in 1998
by Faber and Faber Limited
3 Queen Square London WC1N 3AU

Photoset by Parker Typesetting Service, Leicester
Printed in England by Clays Ltd, St Ives plc

A CIP record for this book
is available from the British Library
ISBN 0-571-19644-6

2 4 6 8 10 9 7 5 3 1

CONTENTS

Introduction:
Boaz Yakin in conversation with Oren Moverman, vii

A PRICE ABOVE RUBIES, I

Boaz Yakin

VIRTUE IN WRITING
A conversation with Boaz Yakin
● OREN MOVERMAN

When I first called Boaz Yakin about doing an interview for the Faber publication of his new screenplay *A Price Above Rubies*, he suggested I send him the questions in writing. 'There's something about the page,' he explained, 'something about sitting down and filling up that space that makes total sense to me. I don't think I can express myself verbally as well as I can on the page.' Well, I was not willing to let him off the hook that easily; as much as the writer delights in seeing his words on the page, the interviewer takes pleasure from listening to the writer talk.

Yakin is a seasoned writer who just happens to be a remarkably accomplished director. In 1994 he arrived at the Sundance Film Festival to win the Film-maker's Trophy with his first feature *Fresh*, a carefully constructed, psychologically gripping urban drama about a doomed twelve-year-old black drug peddler (Sean Nelson) who efficiently scams his way out of the control of the drug lords who are shattering the lives of those around him. The film stars Samuel L. Jackson, Giancarlo Esposito and N'bushe Wright, and while it quickly made Yakin one of the leading young directors of the indie generation, few people realized he had already left behind a productive Hollywood screenwriting career.

I sat down with Boaz Yakin one early Saturday morning to talk about the long road traveled to his second feature as a writer/director. A few hours later, he admitted to having had a fairly painless verbal experience.

OREN MOVERMAN: *The first thing I'd like to talk about, in regards to your work, is you. It all starts with your name, really. There's always been some confusion as to who you are, with some people thinking you're African-American, based on the black inner city environment of* Fresh, *others thinking you're Israeli or maybe Muslim.*
BOAZ YAKIN: Well, I was born in New York, but my parents are Israeli; that is, they were born in British Mandate Palestine. My father grew up in Jerusalem; his family moved there in 1895 from Syria. It's actually an interesting family history; I'm not really sure

how it relates to my work, but it must in some way. My great-grandfather was a rabbi in Aleppo (Haleb, Syria). He had a son and then a number of daughters. He wanted another son, and he prayed to God, or so the story goes, that if he had another boy he'd move to Jerusalem. That son was my grandfather – who had a terrible relationship with his older brother and actually left Palestine in his early teens and moved to America. He became a traveling salesman when he was just sixteen, and ended up in Mexico during the Zapatista Revolution and almost got killed there. So he returned to New York, but his older brother came over after running into a lot of trouble in Palestine and my grandfather took him into his haberdashery shop on the Lower East Side. They still had real estate in Palestine and after an earthquake in the twenties, my grandfather went back to evaluate the damage. In Egypt he met my grandmother and they settled in Palestine because they got into terrible debt. So my father grew up in the Thirties in Jerusalem. My mother's parents came from Poland. They moved to Tel Aviv together, but when my mother was two years old, her mother left and moved to Paris just before World War Two. So my mother grew up with a foster family on a farm, with her father visiting frequently. After the war, my mother moved to be with her mother in Paris. My dad went to Paris in the Fifties after his army service. He hated the army and was a terrible soldier, always getting in trouble. He was acting in a theater in Jerusalem and went to study mime with Marcel Marceau. At Marceau's, he met my mother. When their relationship became serious, it turned out my mother had been married when she was eighteen to some crazed Israeli criminal. She divorced him before she went to France, but he was threatening to come over and get my parents, so they ended up coming to the United States with the help of Stella Adler, the great acting teacher, who had met my father in Paris. She got my father over first and he started teaching physical movement for actors with her. Then my mother came over and this is where we've been ever since. My father became a theater director; he teaches still at Juilliard. For years they had a mime company, but they always taught acting. My mother taught physical acting at Circle in the Square, here in New York, and now she is also teaching at Juilliard.

OM: *So you grew up in a somewhat bohemian, artistic environment that blended many cultures?*

BY: I guess I grew up in a schizoid environment. At home I had this artistic family, but my parents sent me to a Yeshiva on 75th Street – a modern orthodox Jewish day school with a mixture of all sorts of types, even some Lubavitch Hassidim. I think my parents just didn't want me to go to public school; they wanted me to speak Hebrew, but they didn't quite realize how religious that education was. It was much less about Hebrew than it was about Judaism. It was also a very conservative environment. So, in a way, I was growing up almost ashamed of my parents, because they were mimes who put on weird make-up and strange shows while my friends' parents wore suits and made money. When you're a kid you don't want to be that different. Also, although I was glad that I wasn't a practicing Jew, that I didn't have to do all that restrictive shit on Saturday, and even though I didn't believe in it from the age of eight, there was still that feeling of embarrassment when everyone else in your school is going to synagogue and they catch you walking around with your McDonald's bag. I had this sense of guilt; I thought I was going to hell because I turned the light on on the Sabbath.

The one thing I remember is this rabbi – who actually helped me on *A Price Above Rubies*, although now he might regret it – who, when we were nine, decided to teach us all the various punishments of the time of the Sanhedrin (the council of the elders in Old Jerusalem). We actually got tested on the issues of choking, stoning, burning – the various techniques. It got very specific. There was all this business about 'Cares'; sort of unknown death that you get from God as punishment. We were told that having leavened bread at home during Passover was a shoe-in for that. Of course, being under thirteen, I knew my parents were responsible for my sins, and I knew I was doing everything wrong. It freaked me out that my dad was going to pay for my actions. I went home crying to my mother and she came to school to talk with the rabbi and he apologized. Then four years later my brother had the same rabbi and he came home crying for the exact same reason.

So it was a strange sort of existence. During the summer we'd go over to France to do a show. It was the Seventies; all of my parents' friends would hang around the house. And, of course, I enjoyed all the cosmopolitan aspects of that life, but then I would come back home to school and it was this other world.

After one year of Yeshiva high school, I said, 'Fuck this!' I went to the Bronx High School of Science, which was another mistake because I hated science and math. I should have gone to study music and art. I had the worst years of my life in high school. I hated it, I thought it was never going to end. But once I got to college things fell into place.

OM: *Did film have any important place in your childhood?*
BY: I loved movies, I was generally in love with storytelling. The movie that influenced me most growing up was probably *The Adventures of Robin Hood* with Errol Flynn. It presented me with a character that I idolized; someone who is a part of a certain society, but is also an outsider, who knew how to rise above it all, knew right from wrong on his own terms. I guess I've incorporated some of these character traits into Fresh and Sonia Horowitz. Then in high school, when I was fourteen, I saw *Kagemusha* and recognized, for the first time, that there was a vision behind the film, that there was a director running the show. Kurosawa really altered my understanding of film and I wanted to get serious about directing. So when I got to college, I took a lot of film courses. I moved over from City College in Harlem to NYU downtown, where I spent only a year. While I was there, I felt very pressed to become a director. There was a two-day practical course about how to get jobs in the film industry. The teacher talked about contacting production companies and working as an intern, and I was sitting there thinking, 'You must be mad!' So after class I asked him, 'What do you really do to become a movie director?' He was nice enough to take me to dinner, and essentially told me that a lot of directors get there by writing their own scripts. So I went off and over the second semester of my sophomore year I wrote a script – an action type thing. Over that summer I sent the script to an agent who liked it a lot and actually found a producer to option it. And that agent urged me to leave school and go to Hollywood to work as a professional screenwriter. He was a hot-shot agent at the time and he said he could get me jobs. So I did it. I moved to California and it was

kind of scary. He didn't let me show anyone the second script I wrote because he didn't think it was good enough. I ended up writing a script for United Artists and then another; I was working as a professional writer, but none of my stuff got made.

OM: *Yet it sounds as if the transition from second year film student to professional Hollywood writer was relatively smooth for you.*
BY: Look, I was lucky. I came in before the concept of the million-dollar screenplay hit and everyone and their grandmother was writing a script. There was still this idea of looking for new talent in Hollywood. Action movies had just gotten big and I wrote an action script. I know a hundred, thousand million percent that if I came up today with that first script I wrote, I wouldn't be able to get an agent. I remember this agent calling me on the phone and yelling, 'You're a genius, a genius', but I had enough presence of mind to know what that meant.

OM: *How did you fit into the Hollywood environment?*
BY: I didn't. I was twenty years old, with no life experience, and I had to try to make it in this grinding mill where this producer was calling me his adopted son one day and then never returning my calls. I was making money, I didn't have to pay these ridiculous film school tuitions, and I got to learn and get some experience. But I knew I had to pull myself out of there. After three years a script of mine, *The Punisher*, got made. It was completely rewritten by the producer, but it paid a lot of bills. And then my friend Scotty and I wrote *The Rookie*, which was picked up by Warner Brothers. By that time I was so miserable in Los Angeles, so unhappy, that I knew I was leaving. I picked up *Tropic of Cancer* and *Tropic of Capricorn* and had all of my suspicions about what a wasted life is about confirmed. I knew Paris was the place to go and realign my brain. I stuck around just long enough to watch Clint Eastwood direct *The Rookie*, which was very important for me to do because I got to watch how a crew works, how a set is run; I got to get into his head as a director. It was a great learning experience for me.

OM: *What did you learn from Eastwood?*
BY: Well, he's a spur-of-the-moment type of director. He doesn't

even look at what a set is going to be like before he shows up. He arrives, looks around, decides what to shoot and that's it. When he's excited, he gets some really good things. When he's tired – which was most of the time on *The Rookie* because they were shooting nights, long hours and he was also acting in the film – he gets television-type results. So I learned about the necessity for planning for those days when you may not be on the ball. Because he was a spontaneous creator – he wasn't shooting storyboards or anything like that – I got to see him working out every scene right there. Halfway through the shoot, I could already tell where he was going to put the camera next; I really got a sense of what he was doing. It was an amazing education for me. It grounded me in the practical aspects of how to transform those pictures you see in your head into a movie. Then I got the fuck out of Los Angeles.

In Paris I wrote a novel, I argued a lot with my brother – who kept telling me I should do better things, and he was right – and then I got a call from Lawrence Bender, who's been a friend all throughout the L.A. years. He told me about *Reservoir Dogs*, which he had just produced for Quentin Tarantino, and he said that if I wrote a script for a reasonable budget, he would be able to get it made. That's how *Fresh* was born.

OM: *Was your approach to writing* Fresh *any different from that of your Hollywood scripts?*
BY: My artistic approach was different, my goal was different – I was finally going to direct – but the overall process was the same. Of course, my grasp of structure, character and dialogue was inferior when I was in Hollywood, but I was very young then and I was writing action movies. What I tend to do with a script is come up with a character, or a situation which that character is in. Then I start researching the environment and it's really through the research that my mind is most open to constructing the story. While I'm interviewing people, going places, seeing things, everything starts to come in and feed my mind, until I feel I have enough related and unrelated notes to put everything together into a story. Then I just put it on paper.

OM: *You integrate very specific camera directions into the story in both* Fresh *and* Rubies. *Is it because you are the director in both cases or have you always done that?*
BY: I try to give a screenplay not only the story itself, the dialogue, but also a sense of pacing, energy and focus within the scene. There are moments when a moving camera isn't just a camera in motion, it's actually something that puts a point across. I specify camera directions when I feel it's necessary for the reader's perception of what I'm writing. I use them only to help the reading experience; they direct the reader to see the film in a similar fashion to the way it will be shot. Screenplays are weird. It's a reading experience, yet when people read your script – people like studio executives – they fully expect to read it in one sitting and not be bored for an hour and thirty minutes; it's supposed to approximate the experience of watching a movie. So you're always under pressure to tell an interesting story, but also to tell it in a way that most accurately conveys the experience of later seeing it as a finished product. My scripts used to look like novels, I would overwrite and that would slow everything down. Now I see that the best model for screenwriting, though not necessarily the best writer, is Hemingway – clear, clean, dramatically focused sentences, conveying image but without an overabundance of words. As a screenwriter, you are writing for the reader; you try to let words flow on the page, but sometimes the danger is getting married to directions that may not work when you actually rehearse and work on the scene.

OM: *How did you come up with the character of Fresh?*
BY: I think he came from writing action films in Hollywood. At that time the big heroes were Schwarzenegger and Stallone – big, muscular, confident guys who were smashing everything up. I just asked myself who would be the most powerless person you could possibly imagine. And the answer, of course, was a kid. I wanted to put a kid in a situation that an action hero would have to deal with. The film that influenced me the most with this character was Kurosawa's *Yojimbo*. I loved the interplay of double-crossings in that film, but Yojimbo is ultimately a tough superhero that you never really worry about. I thought that if I did that kind of story with a kid, it would be really interesting. And at the time no one,

except Spike Lee, was really doing black movies and I thought it would be interesting to do a film in that environment.

I did a lot of reading, trying to understand the historical background. And then, after putting things in a historical context, I was ready to experience the present; so I went to the neighborhoods. I spent a lot of time in Brooklyn schools interviewing kids, which was the most valuable thing for me. I did a screenwriting workshop with some kids in the South Bronx, and got to know kids, got to talk to them and hear their voices. Of course, at the end of the day I was making it up, but I was grounding it in reality.

OM: *Did it occur to you that it might be controversial for a white film-maker to make a crime film about the so-called black ghetto?*
BY: Not really. When I started the process, people were telling me I'd never get financing for a movie about black people because no one wanted to see that stuff. While I was researching *Fresh, Boyz N the Hood* came out, so when the script was done, every company we went to was telling us, 'We already have our black movie in development right now.' So the climate changed within a year. I thought the story might be controversial, but I didn't realize initially that my skin color was a big deal. To me, using a society that seems very specific, like Fresh's neighborhood, or Hassidic society in *Rubies*, is essentially a metaphor for living in whatever environment you live in; it's a metaphor for the world around you, it avoids the vagueness of generalizations. When you can pick an environment that is clearly defined, the character's conflict with that environment becomes much sharper.

OM: *There was real anger in some reviews, and at the Sundance screening some people were very upset. As a white person living in a racially divided country, you are not supposed to have any insight into that world.*
BY: Look, if a white person made a film called *Menace II Society* and showed scenes in which black kids sit around watching snuff films without one person in the room saying, 'Yo, guys, this is sick,' no one would have treated it as a legitimate social statement. He would have been lynched. *Fresh* never went in that direction. To me, the characters in the film have pathos and dignity. But

because I was white and I was presenting a world that focused on crime and the negative aspects of the experience, I think people were irritated.

OM: *There's always this issue about film-makers working outside their culture, not working from their own experience. From Renoir in* The River *to Ang Lee in* The Ice Storm.

BY: Part of the fun of living in the United States is being surrounded by a wide variety of cultures. Sometimes being from outside a culture enables you to pick up on things that people inside take for granted. I think it's valuable to have an outsider perspective. More than anything else, people don't like to be criticized by people who are not a part of their culture. I guess no one likes to feel they are being criticized, period. Especially people who have suffered for hundreds of years. It works both ways, when Spike Lee made *Mo Better Blues*, he had two unsympathetic Jewish characters in it and there was a huge uproar. If I was not Jewish, *A Price Above Rubies* would have people screaming anti-Semitism from here till next Shabbas. The way it stands now, some people may want to accuse the writer of being a self-hating Jew. And believe me, I couldn't be further from a self-hating Jew, but people who are paranoid about these things will always have those claims. One of the reasons I like to do these films about cultures that aren't necessarily my own is that I'm learning, it's my way of staying interested in a life. If I was just going to write about people living in my neighborhood on the Upper West Side of New York, I would die of boredom. I never liked school, but I love researching and learning about other people, finding their universality or their particularities. As much as I am making movies to entertain someone else, I am also doing it to keep me growing, to entertain me.

OM: Fresh *reads like a writer's film, character-driven, tightly woven, the sort of thing an inexperienced director could work into a brilliant film, or screw up completely. How did it feel to be in the spotlight in the pressurized role of the director? Was it a comfortable transition?*

BY: I started out feeling very comfortable, but it turned into a very hard shoot for me. I didn't have the kind of support that I needed. I knew very clearly what I wanted, and I think people didn't expect a first-time director to be a hundred percent confident and they were put out by it. I was also younger and pretty intense. I was probably suited to directing artistically, but not temperamentally. I don't like being the boss, I don't like being in charge that much, and I sure don't like being a cheerleader, so after a shot was done I would just be standing there, thinking about the next shot, not realizing everyone is looking at me thinking something is wrong.

I didn't realize, when I was directing, that every little mood switch affects everybody else on set. You really have to take on that role of 'The Director' in a low-budget film so that everyone can feel they are a part of a team. The shoot went well, but it was very tense and I didn't really enjoy it. I enjoyed working with the actors, I loved the kid Sean, but I found the whole experience very emotionally draining and, when it was all done, I thought I didn't want to direct again. And to tell you the truth, I prefer writing. Even after directing my second film, which was a better experience, where everyone really felt together, I can honestly say I don't like directing. I don't like having to convince people to do things for me, I don't like having to talk actors into playing certain things, I don't like having to figure out their psychology so that I'm not making a mistake, upsetting them. I just don't like it. I don't like having just two weeks to rehearse and having to push for results because there's no time. I don't like being the general. I can't figure out how some directors, the Oliver Stones of the world, are able to march on to the set and crank out these big films every eighteen months. The two small films that I've made up to now were so difficult.

OM: *Then why are you continuing to direct?*
BY: The whole *auteur* theory doesn't mean anything to me, but a director does shape a film, and being just a screenwriter is less gratifying. If I'm going to write a film, I might as well work hard to make it look and sound and feel the way it was intended. And that also means working every day with the editor, really reworking the film in the editing room. I don't understand how some directors can make a film and then just pass it on to the editor. As creative as the editor is, it's the director's job to be there for every frame, every cut. I also think a lot of directors don't even know what they want a performance to look like, what style and tone they want the

actor to convey based on the screenplay. So as long as I'm in the business of film, I need to direct, but if I ever get the feeling that it isn't worth it, then I'll just stop writing screenplays, I'll write fiction.

OM: *Both your films as a director are urban dramas. Your cinematographer, Adam Holender, seems to be the perfect partner for your big city sensibilities. He shot* Midnight Cowboy, Panic in Needle Park, Street Smart, Smoke *and more.*
BY: When we were in pre-production for *Fresh*, I kept talking about this Seventies style I wanted the film to have, a texture not unlike *Midnight Cowboy*. Finally, it occurred to me to ask if the guy who shot *Midnight Cowboy* was still alive. It turned out he was only twenty-eight when he shot the film. He's an amazing pro, very meticulous. He was incredibly helpful on every level, combining shots, knowing exactly what we could get. When it came to *Rubies*, I wanted the film to be mostly interiors. Like Ibsen's *A Doll's House*; I wanted it to feel like you were always on the inside, as if it was a staged play. I wanted the light to be very rich and textured; I was less concerned with the shots, the look mattered to me more. So I designed the look and shot list to fit Adam's strengths, the long takes that he loves so much, the movement in the frame. It was even more collaborative than *Fresh*.

OM: *Knowing what we now know about your process, I assume* A Price Above Rubies *started with the central character, Sonia Horowitz. What drew you into the Hassidic environment this time?*
BY: I was working on a script called *Flying*, which was about homeless people living in New York. The main character was a Pentecostal preacher living on the streets. A social worker told me about a Hassidic homeless guy, I think his nickname was Kosher Dave, or something like that. He was a Lubavitch guy who was still carrying the Grand Rebbe's picture with him.

OM: *That's very unusual. The Hassidic community is known for taking care of its poor.*
BY: That's true, but he was a sex addict. He'd run around on his wife and kids, spent a lot of energy on hookers, until finally he was thrown out of the community. I liked the character and wrote him

into the script, but I had too many men already and so I turned him into a woman. I liked the idea of a very sexual Hassidic woman who couldn't take it anymore and was on the streets, wandering. And that woman became Sonia, a character in *Flying*. But I couldn't get that film made, the script was too ambitious and I needed to write something small. Yet I couldn't quite do that. I ended up going to Israel where I wrote this gigantic screenplay about my family in the Forties. Once again, I was stuck with an ambitious project I couldn't get made. But while I was writing this semi-biographical Israeli script, I managed, for the first time really, to write a good female character, based on my aunt who came from Italy. I always wanted to do something with Sonia's character, but I guess I really needed to do something else before I felt comfortable enough to tackle a lead female character.

OM: *Fresh is very much a movie made by an outsider about an insider finding his way out of a community. In a way,* Rubies *is the same because you're a secular Jew who does not have an insider's perspective on Hassidim and you take Sonia out of the only life she knows.*
BY: I think it's deeper than just Fresh and Sonia finding their way out of their communities in films done by an outsider. I see Fresh as a kid who is partly in the community and partly observing it – that's that whole business with the chess games. He's one of the kids in the hood, but he's also watching them, he can get detached and be somewhere else. So he is not a complete insider. Sonia isn't removed emotionally, the way Fresh is, but she also has this other world in which she lives, symbolized by the ghosts, her brother, Yossi, her overwhelming passion.

OM: *Do you think that's somehow connected to who you are?*
BY: I grew up feeling like I am half in the world and half out of it. And I don't think it has to be tied to a specific culture. I've always felt like part of me is standing in a room talking to somebody, and the other part of me is watching a film of me standing in a room talking to somebody. Anyone who wants to say I am out of the culture of Fresh, may be totally correct, but I know that guy, I know the character because he is a person who doesn't want to feel. When his stability is threatened, he decides to kill anything that is making him feel. The violence that is instigated by Fresh at

the end of the film is his way of destroying the things that are making him feel pain. At the end, he destroys what made him feel, but he realizes he can't destroy his own pain. *Rubies* is different because Sonia desperately wants to feel, but she's stuck in an environment where she is not encouraged to have emotions. I think when you're younger, you fight feelings, you want to be tough and independent. As you get older, you find your own feelings. But in both cases, they are characters who are already outsiders from the very beginning. It's too bad I couldn't get *Flying* made, because that was really the emotional transition from *Fresh* to *Rubies*.

OM: *The Hassidic environment you chose for* Rubies *is not the esoteric, mystical one of, say, Sidney Lumet's* A Stranger Among Us. *This particular sect, like Lubavitch, is more integrated into society, more American, less hidden, even in terms of language. This makes Sonia's journey into the secular world – as unique as it is – less extreme.*
BY: The first person who helped me with the research was an ex-Satmar Hassid. Satmars are much more extreme and isolated from American life, even though they are so close to it physically. All of my original research was on the Satmar way of life. But then I realized, I'd never get anywhere with them once I needed to talk to them, because they are closed off. I told my brother about my frustration with that and he suggested I drop the idea of a closed-off sect because it would make the characters really difficult to understand. And then it hit me that the story would be more interesting if I based it on people who are not that far removed from everyday life. If Sonia was Satmar, it would have been too easy to present that life as a harsh reality for a woman. It's like making a prison movie. It would have been a social statement about a society that is hard on women. But I was more interested in the personal story. The Lubavitch style of life is actually very warm; there are a lot of restrictions, it's a conservative society, but it's not an insanely conservative society to me. I found it psychologically more interesting to tell a story that wasn't black and white. In this environment, it became much more about the needs of the personal against the needs of the group.

OM: Fresh *is set in a more 'realistic' domain than* Rubies, *which is really a fable. It looks as if you've now started experimenting with a more 'magic realist' approach. The appearance of Yossi, the dead brother, throughout the film, the mysterious beggar woman, even the opening story about a soul caught between this world and the next one – are these elements in the film just because of the religious subject matter of* Rubies, *or is it a stylistic preference you've developed in your writing?*

BY: I always leaned toward that. Even in *Fresh*, I tried to work in little things like the music not being very realistic, or true to the milieu, or those weird visions when Fresh sees the train tracks. Someone told me after the Sundance screening of *Fresh*, that he saw it as a fairy tale about a prince trying to rescue a princess in a castle. I really wanted to have a poeticized tone under the realism of *Fresh*. In *Rubies*, I just decided to push more in that direction.

I feel that this approach more accurately reflects human experience than a 'realistic' approach. We spend half our lives focusing on what's in front of us, and the other half day-dreaming. Also, a film is a story, it is fake, it isn't real. By adding these 'unrealistic' elements, I feel you make a film more emotionally accessible. *Drugstore Cowboy* is a perfect example. You leave that film feeling you've experienced a very real exploration of a person's way of seeing the world; you get Matt Dillon's character's emotional life because all these weird visions in the film are insights into his imagination, into his mind. It takes away many realistic pretenses, but you are allowed a kind of access to a character that you couldn't get just from seeing his actions and hearing his words.

OM: *There's a confusing moment in the film where the 'real' and the 'magical' worlds meet. Sonia is sitting on a bench with who we perceive to be the ghost of her brother. But the mysterious beggar woman we perceive to be real interacts with him as well as her.*

BY: It's confusing, but to me that's the crux of it all. The whole thing is a story, none of it is real. The confusion has to do with viewers trying to bring the film to their experiential level, rather than hop into the experience of the film. When a film declares, 'You are now entering Oz', people go with it, but when a film looks more 'realistic' and the characters are of the recognizable world,

xx

people try to relate it more to their own lives. I never treat the beggar as 'real' and so she can have all these interactions.

OM: *How did the script change in the actual making of the film?*
BY: This script went through more drafts than usual. Once we got into rehearsal, the script changed somewhat, particularly the scenes between Sonia and Ramon. The story is about a woman searching and not quite knowing where she's going; the script needed to find its way toward the way Renee Zellweger was seeing it. A few scenes at the end made her look weaker than we wanted, and Renee was very helpful in taking away self-pity from the way the character was written. As a writer, I am glad to let things from the script go if it makes the film better. The collaboration with the actor always wins. Sometimes things just don't sound the way you hear them in your head.

OM: *Although you put your characters in specific environments, you seem to search for traits that would defy stereotypes. In* Rubies, *Mendel, who could have been presented as a bitter, betrayed zealot, is able not only to take responsibility for his son, but also to accept his wife's otherness. Even Sender, who could have been purely an exploiter and a monster, is turned into a strange sort of liberator.*
BY: Well, I've been accused of writing characters who are stereotypes, especially in *Fresh* where blacks and Hispanics are drug dealers. But I don't think my critics were ever looking at the humanity of the characters. I'm interested in allowing characters to be more than one thing, even though they are mainly one thing. Mendel is the most important character in the film – other than Sonia – because he represents the best of what that world has to offer. He's not what she needs, but he is a *tzaddik* (righteous man). I wanted to show what I think a real *tzaddik* is able to do, which is to be generous even to that which he cannot fit into his world. That's where Mendel is able to rise above what's expected of him in the Hassidic world, above the stereotype. And Sender, I think, is sort of a jerk, but he is the first to recognize Sonia's passion. He should have been able to do what Sonia does at the end of the film, but he lacked the courage to get out of that environment, so he ended up twisting it. I think that a character like Sonia, who is so entrenched in a certain way of looking at

xxi

herself, at a certain way of looking at the world around her, and the way the world looks at her, sometimes needs to get fucked by life before she can gain some measure of control over it. So Sender symbolizes that life force, the thing that rapes you and doesn't show you any compassion, but ultimately breaks the first wall around you and enables you to look differently at the world. The next step in her evolution is getting some handle on life. I tried to show her being jarred into awareness through Sender, and then ultimately define those things which she doesn't want in her life. At the end of the film, she doesn't quite know what she wants, she only knows what she doesn't want. That's a huge step in the evolution of a character. So, Sender is really life. And Ramon is the continuation of her feelings for her brother; when she sees his art, his jewelry, she sees the beauty, the passion she had been looking for in herself.

OM: *The film separates the world into two opposing forces, on the one side beauty, art, love and passion – which are all classically looked upon as feminine traits – and on the other side there is religion, laws, codes, morality – all patriarchal constructs. You even take it into a speech in which God is described as the old bully and the devil is described as wise and beautiful. The Rebbitzn's 'thank you' monologue addresses this conflict directly, the idea of human love and passion being stronger than the worship of God and the laws of the community. It all ties in together.*

BY: So much of organized religion is designed around male terror of feminine sexuality. So much of it is about man's fear of losing his self control because of the way women make him feel. Essentially, it comes down to a fear of being aroused that makes Islam drape its women and Hassidim stress modest clothing and head covers. To me, the first half of the film is a behavioral comedy about a feminine sexuality that goes out of control in a situation where it must be put in its place. I tried to present this kind of world where Sonia's sexuality is ruining all the stability around her.

In the second part of the film, there's this coming to terms with the strengths of her own femininity within the confines of the patriarchy. It's not about good and evil. We talk about God and the devil because those are the figures that are given to us, but there were female deities long before the Jews' concept of Yaweh ever came into existence. And there is this other side that is as beautiful and as ancient as the concept of a patriarchal God, but has essentially got bullied by the Judeo-Christian ethos. What I tried to do with Sonia is give her a sense of her self that is separate from all that is male, that has a different energy.

OM: *How did you approach the casting of* Rubies.
BY: I saw Renee in *The Whole Wide World* and I was very impressed. This was before *Jerry Maguire*, when she was still relatively unknown. She had this amazing ability to convey everything she was feeling without seeming to act. I really liked the idea of giving the role to an actress we haven't seen before; she felt very fresh for me. At that time, we'd already brought on Chris Eccelston to play Sender, and so it was really Mendel we were missing and I felt that we needed a Jewish actor to play such a purely Jewish role. Glen Fitzgerald came in on the first day and I couldn't believe how that Irish poet in him translated into a Hassid. He gave an amazing reading and that was it, three Hassidic Jews all played by non-Jews. I gave them a lot of material to read and we had a woman who was from that world, but had already left it, who took them around the neighborhoods and had them meet some families. We had an excellent dialogue coach who worked very hard with Renee, who's from Texas, and Chris, who's from Manchester. Glen is from Brooklyn so he had less of a problem.

OM: Rubies *is your second Brooklyn film where Manhattan serves as a symbolic foreign island. Are you working on a Brooklyn trilogy?*
BY: That's an accident, believe me. I'd never even been to Brooklyn before I started working on *Fresh*. It's one of those things. There's no design behind it, it wasn't planned. The next film I'll be doing is in the South. It's a horror film set in the Pentecostal world. It's a religious horror film, not supernatural. It deals with the devil and God, a dark satire of fundamentalist attitudes where the devil is the good guy. I guess it's just a wacky movie, much bigger than *Fresh* and *Rubies*. But you know, from my experience, I shouldn't say this is my next film, you never know what you can get made. You can only hope.

A Price Above Rubies

A little girl's face fills the screen. Her name is Sonia. Her eyes are wide – excited and frightened all at once – as she listens intently to the sound of a young Boy's Voice:

> BOY'S VOICE
> (*off-screen*)
>
> A hundred years ago, in a *shtetl* near Pinsk, a young girl ran off into the woods. Her father wanted her to marry a scholar from the Pinsker Yeshiva, but for some reason – maybe she was a little crazy, who knows? – she didn't want to. Anyhow, she ran away.

> SONIA
>
> She ran away from home?

> BOY'S VOICE
> (*off-screen*)
>
> Yeah. It was in the middle of winter . . .

IMAGE: *A white, snowy landscape. Droves of snow falling. A tiny, dark figure wanders into the endless white expanse.*

> . . . and she wandered into the forest. At first no one at home even knew she ran away. They thought she got lost in the snow somewhere and died. They looked and looked for her, but they never found her body. They decided the wolves ate her up. So they quit looking . . .

The tiny figure is gone, leaving only a white screen. The Boy's Voice breaks into a painful hacking cough.

Little Sonia sits up and reaches over to her brother Yossi, a pale, sickly looking boy whose gaunt face is framed by wispy payes. *They are sitting together in the same bed. Sonia hugs her brother, trying to get his coughing to stop . . .*

> SONIA
>
> *Shhh!* Yossi! They'll hear us . . . *Yossi.*

3

Yossi stifles his coughs, slowing his breathing . . .

They'll kill us if they find you here.

> YOSSI
> No, they'll just kill me. I'm your older brother, so it falls on
> me. I'm the only one around here who's gonna die.

Sonia holds him tightly.

> SONIA
> I can't go to sleep without you. I love you more than anything
> – more than Papa or Imma. More than anything.

> YOSSI
> More than God?

> SONIA
> A million times more.

> YOSSI
> You're a sinner. You're supposed to love God above
> everything – and after that, your father and mother. The
> Toyre doesn't even say anything about brothers and sisters.

SONIA

Then we'll add it in.

YOSSI

You can't *add* anything to the Toyre, dunce. It's finished. It's the word of God, and that's that. Not even the greatest scholar can change a letter of it.

SONIA

Then we'll write our own Toyre.

Yossi looks at his little sister for a moment. He smiles. Then he begins again.

YOSSI

It was the longest, hardest winter anyone could remember . . .

IMAGE: *White screen, filled with snow.*

They sat *shiva* in Pinsk for the girl who had disappeared –
And everyone went on with their business. Until, one day . . .

A dark figure appears through the driving snow, and begins approaching . . .

(*off-screen*)

. . . just as suddenly as she had vanished, the girl came back into town. It was the same girl, for sure, but she seemed different – and people could hardly believe it was her. She was also, you know, carrying a baby in her stomach. She was pregnant. But when they checked her, they said she hadn't been with a man . . .

SONIA
(*off-screen*)

Checked? What does that mean? And what do you mean been with a . . .?

YOSSI
(*off-screen*)

Look, I don't know, okay? It's just how I heard them tell it . . .

The figure is drawing nearer, a formless back-lit silhouette, growing larger and darker.

> . . . she had a baby in her stomach, but she didn't have a man. In Pinsk they said she got lost in the forest and was saved by a Demon who made her his wife . . .

The figure has entirely filled the screen, which is now completely black.

SONIA
(off-screen)

What kind of Demon?

YOSSI
(off-screen)

No one knows. They said he had skin black as coal, and eyes green like a cat. And that he was a son of Satan himself . . .

BACK ON: *Sonia covering her mouth with her hands.*

> That spring the woman had a baby – a baby girl. They called her Yitta.

SONIA

Baba Yitta?

YOSSI

That's right. Our whole family is descended from Baba Yitta. All of us. That's why we have such a strong evil urge in us . . . why you and me always sleep in the same bed, even though we shouldn't.

Sonia shakes her head in denial. Yossi nods.

> It's why you don't love God, and talk about changing the Toyre. You don't watch out . . . you're gonna end up just like her.

SONIA

Like how?

YOSSI

When she was real old, and finally died, Baba Yitta went up to heaven – But God didn't want her. So he sent her down to hell. But when she got there, Satan recognized her as his

6

niece. He couldn't bring himself to make her suffer in hell –
so he sent her back up here, to our world, where she wanders
the earth like Cain, alone forever.

Tears well in little Sonia's eyes . . .

> SONIA
> Poor Baba Yitta.

> YOSSI
> Don't cry. Look . . .

*Sonia follows his gaze to the clock by the bedside. Its hands are at
midnight.*

> Remember what day it is?

*Sonia's expression suddenly brightens . . . She turns back to Yossi, who
is now holding a tiny rolled-up cloth in his hand.*

> Happy birthday.

*Sonia takes the cloth and unrolls it – revealing a glittering red stone in
its folds. Her eyes open wide.*

> SONIA
> A *ruby*.

> YOSSI
> I bought it from Papa's shop, with my savings.

*Sonia takes it in her fingers, holding it up to the light . . . then her
expression sinks.*

> SONIA
> It's fake.

Yossi is silent.

> It's the fake one Papa took out of that ring. He was gonna
> throw it out.

*She looks accusingly at Yossi, who drops his eyes. Then Sonia turns,
leans over the edge of the bed, and tosses the stone right down the
heating vent in the floor. She sits up and faces the wall.*

Yossi gets up off the bed and walks over to the window, looking out into the night. He starts taking off his shirt.

Sonia turns and looks at him, her anger giving way to nervousness . . .

Hey . . . what are you doing?

YOSSI

I'm going out to the lake.

Sonia sits up, alarmed . . .

SONIA

Yossi . . . you're not supposed to. Imma said with your asthma you could choke up and . . .

YOSSI

I'm the only boy around here who can't swim. I've been watching everybody else, and I know what to do.

Sonia stands up, as Yossi pulls off his pajama pants, standing in his underwear.

SONIA

No one's even gonna be there to see you swim. They won't know you did it, anyway – so what's the point?

YOSSI

You'll know.

He pads over to the bedroom door and gently opens it, looking out on to the back porch. The sound of crickets fills the room.

SONIA

Yossi! Please don't go!

Yossi looks back and smiles at his little sister. Then he steps out into the night. The sound of the crickets grows louder and louder . . .

Sonia runs across the room and stands by the doorway, hissing urgently:

Yossi . . .

EXT. WOODS – NIGHT

ANGLE ON *the dark outdoors – as Yossi's pale body vanishes into the night . . .*

CUT TO:

A young woman's face contorted and red, cheeks wet with tears, as she cries:

>   YOUNG WOMAN
> *Yossi!*

WIDE ON: *a bright hospital room where the woman is in the process of giving birth, assisted by a Doctor and two Nurses . . .*

>   DOCTOR
> Come on, Mrs Horowitz . . . just a little more . . . one more
> push . . .

CLOSE ON: *the young woman, who is Sonia, now in her early twenties. She grimaces, giving a final effort - then collapses back on to her pillow in a daze. There is the sound of an off-screen smack, followed by a baby's cries . . .*

HOLD ON *Sonia's face, as the baby is lowered into the frame beside her . . .*

>   DOCTOR
>   (*off-screen*)
> Congratulations, Mrs Horowitz. It's a boy.

Sonia looks at her baby through half-conscious eyes, unable to move.

> You were calling out the name 'Yossi', Mrs Horowitz. Is that
> the name you'd like to give your son?

Sonia can't answer . . . Tears fill her eyes and she begins to sob. But these are not tears of joy - they are tears of sorrow . . .

CUT TO:

INT. BAIS AARON SYNAGOGUE/FOYER – DAY

The baby cries his eyes out, as Sonia presses him tightly to her bosom. They are surrounded by a crowd of Hassidic Women, heads covered by

wigs, hats and kerchiefs. Sonia looks through the doorway into the
besmedresh – *the main prayer area –*

INT. *BESMEDRESH* – SONIA'S POV

A throng of Hassidic Men in black suits, open-collared white shirts and slanted black fedoras. All save the very young are bearded, but only a few sport payes.

A Moel – the rabbi who is going to perform the circumcision – stands on the dais and tests the sharpness of his knife by cleanly slicing a thin leather strap with it.

ANGLE ON: *the doorway.*

Sonia blanches, squeezing her baby so hard it screams . . .

Sonia's Mother, a sad-eyed woman who looks far older than her fifty years, reaches over and relaxes Sonia's arms.

> MOTHER
> Easy, Sonia . . . you're turning my only grandchild into a
> tube of toothpaste.

> SONIA
> He's like a sacrifice . . . they're gonna sacrifice my baby.

> MOTHER
> If your father, *zichrono librucha*, wasn't already in his grave.
> you'd put him in it with this spectacle you're making of yourself.
> Shimmie's gonna be just fine. Look out there – every one of
> those men had the same thing, and they're perfectly normal.

> SONIA
> *Normal . . . ?*

ANGLE ON: *the throng of men, a sea of black, swaying in all directions as they pray fervently . . .*

> SONIA
> (*off-screen*)
> They all stand around while some old butcher hacks off my
> baby's *pischke*, and you call them normal? Not today. Not my
> baby . . .

Sonia turns and starts to push through the knot of women, but she is held fast by:

Rachel Feinberg, Sonia's sister-in-law, a beautiful woman in her late twenties.

> RACHEL
>
> My brother told me he married a smart girl, he said he married a pretty girl, but he never told me he married such a chicken. You should be proud, Sonia. This is the moment your son becomes a Jew.

Sonia grimaces, attempting to compose herself.

> SONIA
>
> But does it have to hurt so much?

Inside the besmedresh *Mendel Horowitz, Sonia's young husband, is moving among the men squeezed in around the dais, helping them to place a large, ornate chair – 'Elijah's seat' – in the center of the podium. He is pale, sweating and frantic . . .*

The Moel puts down his knife on a white cloth and calls out:

> MOEL
>
> Bring in the boy.

Mendel grabs the Moel by the arm . . .

> MENDEL
>
> *Wait!* It's alright? The . . . it's clean? Sharp, no nicks or . . . You checked? Then double-check! Check again, to make sure that . . .
>> (*wipes his brow, turning to a friend*)
>
> It's hot . . . it's like an oven in here. I don't want my son cooking in this oven. Someone open a window . . .

Sender Horowitz, Mendel's older brother, drags him off the dais. Sender is an intense bear of a man – the opposite of his younger brother in every way: Mendel is soft, unformed and vulnerable; Sender is a pure jolt of raw power.

> SENDER
>
> You've been coming to this schul for twenty-three years,

Mendel, and there have never been any windows here.
Suddenly this morning there's going to be windows?

MENDEL

Isn't that illegal? A fire hazard or something? This place ought
to be condemned – What kind of a building for people *doesn't
have any windows in it?*

*In the foyer Sonia holds on to her baby, as the synagogue's Shamash
steps up to the doorway, holding out a beautifully embroidered white
pillow.*

*Rachel nods at Sonia, who purses her lips, and reluctantly lowers the
baby on to the pillow. She fixes the* Shamash *with a dangerous glare.*

SONIA

Don't you drop him.

The Shamash *swallows hard, then carries the baby on the pillow into
the* besmedresh – *where he hands him off to another man, who hands
him to his neighbor, and so on. In this manner the baby is passed from
hand to hand toward the podium . . .*

(*from the doorway*)
Don't any one of you dare drop him!

Sender and Mendel are standing side by side at the foot of the dais.

SENDER

Nice girl you married.

MENDEL

(*mopping his brow*)
How about the doors? Are the doors open? Maybe we could
get a nice draft going . . .

(*to one of his friends*)
Baruch, can you get us a draft?

BARUCH

A draft of what?

CLOSE ON: *Sender, closely observing the women in the doorway –
particularly Sonia, who is glaring fiercely into the* besmedresh.

MENDEL
(*off-screen*)
Air, Baruch! A draft of *air*, so my son doesn't choke to death
in this . . .

SENDER
She's a fine-looking girl.

MENDEL
Who?

SENDER
Your wife. I'm looking forward to knowing her better – now
that we're gonna be neighbors.

Mendel looks to his older brother, confused.

I talked to Reb Fedder. You got the job teaching at the
Yeshiva in Boro Park. I've already found you an apartment on
45th Street – it's a stone's throw from by me. We'll finally get
you out of the sticks and into the big city.

MENDEL
And . . . the Rebbe . . . I'm going to be close to the Rebbe?

SENDER
Three blocks from the Rebbe's house, that's where you're
gonna be. You'll pray with the Rebbe, you'll hear the Rebbe's
fabrengen every shabbes – you'll be up to your ears with the
Rebbe.

Tears of joy glitter in Mendel's eyes.

MENDEL
Sender . . . I don't know what to say . . .

SENDER
Just that Sender Horowitz always looks out for his family –
especially his favorite kid brother.

*Mendel smiles gratefully, then almost jumps out of his skin . . . as the
pillow carrying his baby is shoved up to his arms. He gingerly takes it,
and looks down at his son with teary eyes . . .*

Mendel.

13

Mendel steels himself, and hands the baby over to his older brother. Sender carries the baby up to the podium, and sits down in 'Elijah's Seat', cradling the baby, as the Moel picks up his knife and begins to recite a blessing . . .

ANGLE ON: *Sonia, looking on in dismay, her arm gripped tightly by Rachel.*

RACHEL

It's easier if you don't watch.

SONIA

If they can do it, I can watch it.

The Moel finishes his prayer, then bends over the baby and lowers the knife.

CLOSE ON: *Mendel.*

As the baby's sharp cry cuts through the air. Mendel's eyes roll up in his head, and he drops down in a dead faint . . .

CUT TO:

EXT. 13TH AVENUE. BORO PARK – DAY

The camera booms down to reveal a bustling avenue lined with countless shops. The sidewalks are crowded, and the two-way street is clogged by a full-fledged traffic jam.

The camera continues descending, until it has reached the windows of a brand-new station-wagon – against which Sonia's face is pressed. Her son is in her arms and her eyes are brimming with excitement.

SONIA

It's fantastic . . . so many different kinds of people . . .

INT. STATION WAGON – DAY

Mendel shrugs, sitting patiently behind the wheel of the slowly moving car.

MENDEL

Fantastic and not so fantastic.

14

SONIA

Why not fantastic?

MENDEL

Lots of people, lots of influences.

SONIA

They could be good influences.

MENDEL

Sometimes good, sometimes not so good.

Sonia shoots Mendel an annoyed look. They grind to a halt behind another car.

SONIA

Go around, *nu.*

MENDAL

There's no room for a car to pass.

SONIA

There's plenty of room for a car – unfortunately we're not in a car, we're in this ridiculous boat.

MENDEL

It's a station-wagon.

SONIA

Who ever heard of a station-wagon for three people? You could fit a family of twelve in this thing.

MENDEL

God willing.

Sonia starts to say something, but bites it back. Mendel turns and looks tenderly at his wife.

Sonia – I know you're still mad at me for naming Shimmie after the Rebbe, but he's our first son, and he should be invested with the highest level of spirituality. We can call our next boy Yossi.

                                VOICE
                            (*off-screen*)
    I don't care what you call him.

Sonia looks over her shoulder:

Yossi, her ten-year-old brother, looking exactly the same *as he did
when she was a little girl, is sitting in the back seat of the car, twisting
one of his* payes *around his finger.*

                                SONIA
                            (*to Yossi*)
    Who asked you?

*Mendel looks at Sonia, confused and hurt. To his eyes, other than them,
there is no one else in the car.*

                               MENDEL
    Sonia, I am his father, after all. Give me a little credit.

*Sonia looks back to Mendel, and softens. He reaches up and touches her
cheek . . . leans over to kiss her . . . then suddenly his attention is
caught:*

*Mendel's POV on the street. A flock of black-garbed Hassidim are
descending the steps of the large synagogue on the adjacent side-street.
They are all pressed in close around a single grey-bearded man, doting
over his every step.*

                               MENDEL
                            (off-screen)
    The Rebbe!

ANGLE ON: *the station-wagon. Sonia is barely able to keep the baby
from hitting the windshield, as Mendel pulls the car around to the side of
the street and hops out.*

EXT. BORO PARK STREET – DAY

Mendel hurries around the car, and bumps right into a schnorrer – *a
bent, old Beggar Woman – clad in tattered, colorful rags. She speaks in
a thick East European accent:*

OLD WOMAN

A few pennies, young rebbe . . . a little change for an old woman who's been too long on her tired feet . . .

Frustrated, knowing he can't morally ignore the Old Woman to get to the Rebbe, Mendel fishes around in his pocket . . . but it's empty.

MENDEL

My wife's carrying all of our money, I'm . . .

The Old Woman squeezes Mendel's arm.

OLD WOMAN

I've been on my feet such a long time, young rebbe. Such a long time . . .

Mendel grits his teeth, then turns back to the car, where Sonia is already leaning out of the window, holding out a dollar bill. Mendel nods gratefully, and runs around the Old Woman – who takes a step toward Sonia.

God bless you and your children . . . a thousand blessings on your house . . .

Her hand almost touches the dollar . . . then she suddenly stops.

SONIA

Don't worry, bubby. It won't bite.

But the Old Woman isn't interested in the dollar any more. It's Sonia's face that she is now studying with her pale, rheumy eyes.

OLD WOMAN

At last.

Sonia blinks. The Old Woman reaches out, and closes Sonia's hand back around the dollar.

God bless you, child.

She turns, and slowly shuffles away . . . Dolly in on Sonia's confused face.

SONIA

For what?

The Old Woman brushes past Mendel, who is standing in the middle of the sidewalk, watching the Rebbe and his entourage pile into several black sedans, which then start up the street.

Mendel turns and looks back at Sonia, his face beaming like a little boy's. He shouts.

MENDEL

The Rebbe!

CLOSE ON: *Sonia. She forces a smile, but her expression is overcast with some kind of grey premonition . . . Mendel's voice comes in over the soundtrack:*

(*voice-over*)

– And so it was that God picked that humble little mountain, Mount Sinai, on which to present His greatest gift . . .

INT. YESHIVA BETH EMETH. CLASSROOM – DAY

Dollying across the faces of a class of six-year-old Hassidic Boys – some sitting in rapt attention, others throwing things at each other, others nearly asleep, as Mendel's voice continues:

MENDEL
(*off-screen*)

. . . the gift of His Toyre. But the question still remained: To who was he going to give such a gift? So God set out to find which amongst the Nations of the earth was worthy of receiving His Toyre. He went to the goyim in Canaan and asked, 'Look what I have here for you – The Toyre! Do you want my Toyre?' And what did the goyim say? Did they want God's Toyre?

ANGLE ON: *Mendel standing at the front of the class, grinning as the kids erupt in a motley chorus of 'No!' and 'No way!' Mendel is animated and alive, a man joyfully in his element:*

Well, they asked first. 'Toyre, eh? Tell us what's in it?'
(*deepening his voice to a godly baritone*)
In the Toyre it is written: *'Thou shalt not steal!'*

18

(*scratching his head; as the goyim again*)
Hmmm. No stealing? Forget it – This Toyre is not for us. No thanks.

The boys titter, grinning at one another, as Mendel continues.

So God went searching some more. Where did he search?

BOYS
(*shouting*)
America! Yisroel! New York! Everywhere!

MENDEL
God came to America, and asked the American goyim: 'Do you want my Toyre?' And they also said, 'Tell us what's in it, first.'
(*voice deepening*)
'*Honor thy father and thy mother.*'
(*as the American goyim*)
Naaaaaaaaah! Respect our parents? I don't think so! Get that thing – whattaya call it? Toyre? Get it out of here!

The boys laugh happily.

From one nation to another God went, always asking: 'Do you want my Toyre?' And always they asked, 'What's in it?' And always he told them: '*Thou shalt not steal. Thou shalt not kill.*' And always they threw it back in God's face. 'No way, José – this *meshugas* is not for us.'
(*pauses, looking over his class*)
So God went to Yisroel. 'Yisroel,' he asked us, 'Jews, do you want my Toyre?' And what did they answer?

All the boys chime in at once, shouting along with their teacher:

BOYS/MENDEL
'*Naaseh ve nishmah!*'

MENDEL
That's right. 'We shall do, and we will listen.' Not 'Tell us what's in it, first, so we can decide if we want it.' *We shall do, and we will listen.* Anything you want us to do, Lord – we

have already accepted it. And now, only now, did God see that He had found in us a people worthy to bear witness, and carry with us his greatest gift – the eternal words of his *Sefer Toyre.*

One of the boys, Heshie, raises his hand. Mendel points at him.

> HESHIE
> My father says it's okay to steal from goyim. He says to steal by goyim isn't really stealing.

Some of the boys laugh. Mendel's expression darkens.

I asked Reb Zvi about it, and he said stealing is stealing, no matter from who. But if he's right, then I can't obey the commandment to honor my father, because one can't honor a thief.

Mendel opens his mouth to offer an answer . . . but he doesn't really have one, so he just stands there, blinking.

CUT TO:

INT. HOROWITZ APARTMENT. KITCHEN – DAY

A selection of square swatches of different fabrics is spread out over the dining table.

> VOICE
> (*off-screen*)
> – It's a vast selection, but a few of the samples cry out for immediate consideration. Like this sweet floral pattern here . . . or this nice blue chiffon look . . .

Sonia and Rachel are standing in the little kitchen in Sonia's new apartment, looking on as Shaindy, a bewigged saleslady, chatters on about the selection. The sound of Rachel's three children tearing around can be heard from the next room.

> SHAINDY
> . . . I'd personally recommend something light and airy to complement the charming atmosphere of your home . . .

SONIA

'Charming' means 'small', right?

SHAINDY

I assume you'll hang curtains in the living-room as well as here in the kitchen, which opens up a whole range of choices – for instance, you could decide on an atmosphere of integration, and unify the space with a single theme; or you could separate the rooms visually – different looks, different atmospheres, different states of mind.

SONIA

After listening to you for half an hour I don't know *what* state my mind is in. I don't even know what language you're talking, you could be talking Chinese, I wouldn't know the difference.

Rachel is in the background, shouting at her kids in the other room.

RACHEL

Quiet down, already! You're wrecking your aunt's new apartment before she's moved into it!

SHAINDY

In one case the apartment is whole, unified. In the other the kitchen is the kitchen and the living-room is the living-room. You're cooking all day, you're exhausted, you walk out of the kitchen and *presto*, it's like you're in another world.

Sonia looks numbly at the saleswoman.

SONIA

One of us here is completely insane. I think it's you, but you're gonna have company real soon if I have to listen to one more word of this *meshugas*.

Tsipi, Rachel's ten-year-old daughter, enters the kitchen awkwardly carrying little Shimmie.

TSIPI

Aunt Sonia, I think Shimmie's hungry.

Sonia picks up her crying baby, and turns to Rachel:

SONIA

Rachele – pick out one of those samples for me, will you? All these complex curtain-choosing theories are too much for me right now.

SHAINDY

You don't have to choose now. I can just leave your favorite selections with you here so that you can devote as much thought to it as you like . . .

RACHEL

You're gonna have to live with it, Sonia, so I think you ought to . . .

SONIA

Just pick one, okay?

SHAINDY

One? So I'm safe in assuming that you've opted for integration?

CUT TO:

INT. HOROWITZ APARTMENT. BEDROOM – MOMENTS LATER

Sonia is alone with her baby. The sound of Rachel's Kids is audible from outside the door, as Sonia unbuttons her blouse and raises Shimmie to her breast . . .

CLOSE ON: *Sonia's face reacting to the intense sensation. Her cheeks flush red . . . She covers her mouth with her hand, trying to maintain her composure . . . but finally it's too much for her, and she pulls the baby away from her breast, causing him to start crying again.*

INT. HOROWITZ APARTMENT. KITCHEN – DAY

Sonia hurries out into the noise, brushing past Rachel and Shaindy.

RACHEL

Sonia?

Sonia picks up the baby's empty bottle from the counter-top, then opens the refrigerator – but there is nothing inside.

Sonia sags against the counter, holding her crying son, as Rachel's Kids run around in the foreground shouting at the top of their lungs.

Are you all right, Sonia?
>   (*no answer*)

I know, it can hurt sometimes.

>   SONIA
It doesn't hurt. It's just too . . . I don't know . . . I don't know.

She hands Shimmie over to Rachel, wincing at the noise and confusion.

CUT TO:

INT. *MIKVEH*. PREPARATION ROOM – DAY

Utter silence. High angle of Sonia soaking in a large white tub. A female Attendant sits on a stool beside the tub, holding Sonia's hand . . .

CLOSE ON: *Sonia's hand as the Attendant goes through her fingers one by one, checking for hangnails, clipping one off when she finds it . . . This is followed by a series of images showing Sonia being prepared for her monthly ritual bath:*

Sonia's wet foot extends out of the water, and the Attendant goes over it with the clippers, toe by toe . . .

Sonia rises from the tub, and the Attendant wraps her in a white towel . . .

CLOSE ON: *Sonia's face as the Attendant wipes off the corners of her eyes with a white cloth . . .*

ANGLE ON: *her back – the towel is lowered, and the Attendant runs her hands over Sonia's skin, searching for loose hairs . . .*

INT. *MIKVEH*. HALLWAY – DAY

Sonia follows the Attendant down a long white hallway, past several other Women standing there, wrapped in white towels, silently whispering prayers . . .

INT. *MIKVEH* ROOM – DAY

CLOSE ON: *the back of Sonia's head. The Attendant's fingers run through her extremely short hair, making sure that there are no knots. Sonia walks down the steps, descending into the ritual bath until she is completely submerged . . .*

CUT TO:

INT. HOROWITZ APARTMENT. BEDROOM – NIGHT

Sonia lies in the bed, under white sheets, in a white nightgown. She relaxes into the mattress, enjoying the feel of it against her body and looks across the room:

Mendel is sitting by his desk, in his pajamas, mouthing the words he is reading from a book.

                    SONIA
Mendel.

He raises a finger without looking up: 'Wait a moment.'

Didn't you pray already?

Mendel nods, closing the book. He turns off the desk-lamp, and walks to the bed.

                    MENDEL
I wasn't praying – I was just learning a little Mishnah.

                    SONIA
Anything good?

Mendel sits down on the bed beside Sonia. He kisses her forehead.

                    MENDEL
It's all good.

Sonia smiles. She cranes her neck and kisses Mendel on the lips . . . but he slows her down. He gently moves her back, then turns to shut off the light near the bed . . .

                    SONIA
Mendel . . .

26

(*he stops*)
Can't we leave it on? Just for a little while? I want to see what we're . . .

MENDEL

Sonia.

Sonia stops talking. Mendel switches off the light, and the room is instantly dark, save for the pale moonlight filtering through the windows.

Sonia reaches for Mendel again, but he is sitting upright, murmuring a prayer with his eyes shut. Sonia sags back on her pillow. Mendel finally finishes his prayers, and slides down into the bed beside Sonia.

Mendel kisses Sonia, and she responds. He rolls on top of her and lifts her nightgown. As they begin to make love, Sonia grows more and more passionate, kissing Mendel's cheeks and biting his neck . . . From his hesitant reactions it's clear that his pleasure is overridden by his discomfort. He moves his face away, and when Sonia begins kissing and clawing at his chest, he stops and pushes her back to the pillow.

Enough . . . Sonia . . . *enough.*

SONIA

Enough what?

MENDEL

Just . . . enough.

He moves off of Sonia, sitting up.

It's indecent.

Sonia stares at him, slightly wild-eyed.

SONIA

Making love to your wife is indecent?

MENDEL

Making love like that is.

He runs agitated fingers through his hair . . .

We aren't here alone, Sonia – we're under the eyes of God.
The Talmud teaches a husband to give his wife pleasure –

27

and I try, God knows I try – but for a man it's different. This is supposed to be a mitzvah – a holy act – and a man is to think exalted thoughts in order to sanctify it . . .
                    (*barely able to contain himself*)
But I *can't do it* with you bringing the lusts of Satan himself roaring out of me with your every touch.

SONIA
And I'm supposed to enjoy this? I'm supposed to enjoy myself knowing you're up there thinking of Abraham and Isaac and the damn Rebbe while we're . . .

MENDEL
God forbid! God forbid you should talk that way about the Rebbe! God forbid!

Sonia stifles another outburst . . . then a coughing sound catches her attention. She turns her head and looks:

A small figure is sitting on the floor across the room, tossing a little metal cube into the air and sweeping four others off the floor, playing a game of 'Five Stones'.

Oh, Sonia . . . I'm sorry. I didn't mean to raise my voice to you . . . I'm sorry . . .

He caresses Sonia's hair, then leans over and gently kisses her again, whispering 'I'm sorry' into her ear as he moves her back on to the bed . . . but as they drop down out of frame we see that there is another figure *still sitting in the bed: a second Sonia.*

Sonia #2 gets up off the bed and walks across the room to where Yossi, her brother, is sitting, tossing his 'stones'. She sits down on the floor next to him.

> SONIA
> Can I play a little?

ANGLE ON: *Mendel kissing Sonia, moving on top of her again, muttering breathily . . .*

> MENDEL
> Of course . . . a little is alright, my darling . . . a little is alright . . .

Yossi looks at his sister, sitting across from him, and a smile spreads across his face . . .

CUT TO:

INT. SENDER'S APARTMENT. DINING-ROOM – NIGHT

Wine being poured into an ornately engraved cup. A hand picks it up, and we pan up to the intense, bearded face of:

Sender Horowitz, as he blesses the shabbes wine.

> SENDER
> Baruch ata Adoynai Eloyhenu melech haoylam, Borei peri hagofen.

He takes a sip of the wine.

CUT TO:

Spoons and forks plunging into a pot of thick chulent *stew. The camera pulls back to reveal a large shabbes table, around which a sizeable contingent of the Horowitz clan is seated. Sender is ensconced at the*

*head of the table – beside him is Feiga, his pleasantly drab-looking wife.
Mendel and Sonia are there, as well as Rachel and her husband
Schmuel – a ruddy-cheeked man whose eyes are magnified by thick
glasses. Children of all ages and sizes are squeezed in wherever they can
fit.*

*Yechiel aged eleven, Sender's oldest boy, is standing and attempting to
deliver a* dvar Torah – *'word from the Bible' – over the tumult of the
rest of the kids.*

YECHIEL
– And so God spared the Moabites, the reason being that
Ruth's family was living among them . . .

SCHMUEL
Ah, but why didn't God just allow her family to survive an
attack? He could have done that, couldn't He?

YECHIEL
The answer to the question is: Of course, God could have
done it - but a young girl needs her mother, and a mother
needs a husband, and the family needs a house, and the
house needs a carpenter, and they need someone to make
their clothes . . .

Rachel forces a spoonful of chulent *into the mouth of one of her
children, overriding his protests:*

RACHEL
You don't have to eat it – just put it in your mouth and chew
a little.

YECHIEL
(*raising his voice to be heard over the din*)
So we see that for Ruth to survive, there was need for a whole
community. It shows us how family is so important, even the
evil Moabites were spared by God because they were needed
in order to bring up Ruth.

*The men bang the table with their hands and congratulate the boy with
cries of* 'Yasher coach!'

SENDER

Yasher coach, son. Keep it up and you'll be a great scholar like your uncle Mendel.

MENDEL

Please, I'm not so great just yet.

Sender and Schmuel groan at Mendel's genuine humility. The women are too busy with the children and the food to pay attention.

SCHMUEL

Modesty is becoming, unless it's false. All I hear at the Yeshiva these days is Mendel said this, Mendel said that. Like the Rambam came to learn by them.

MENDEL

While we're on the subject of the Yeshiva, yesterday one of my students – a young boy – asked me a question I couldn't really answer. His father, he says, says it's okay to steal, as long as you steal from goyim. His teacher told him that stealing from anyone is a sin. So if he agrees with his teacher, he's disrespecting his father – but if he agrees with his father, he's honoring a thief, and is in danger of becoming one himself.

> (*strokes his beard*)

Tough question.

SENDER

Only because you're a scholar.

Every adult at the table looks up at Sender – the women included. Only the kids are oblivious. Sender allows himself to make brief eye-contact with Sonia . . . then he looks back at Mendel.

If it's just an opinion, and the boy disagrees with it, that's all right. You can respect those you disagree with. But if his father really is a thief, then the boy should keep his nose in his own business, so he doesn't have to judge what he doesn't know about.

Mendel meets his brother's intense gaze, slightly puzzled. Then he starts in surprise, as Schmuel bangs on the table beside him and begins singing a shabbes song:

SCHMUEL

Tsur misheloi, mishelo achalnu; barchu emunai, shevanu vehotarnu kidevar Adonai . . .

Some of the kids chime in.

KIDS/SCHMUEL

Hazan, hazan, hazan – Hazan et olamo . . .

Sender breaks into a grin, and joins in on the song as well, followed by Mendel.

CUT TO:

INT. SENDER'S APARTMENT. KITCHEN – NIGHT

Dirty dishes are dumped into a plastic tub filled with water by Feiga. Rachel uncovers several cakes for dessert, warning away her kids by brandishing a knife.

RACHEL

Hey! Those little fingers'll get chopped off if they wander where they don't belong!

Sonia walks in and hands Feiga another stack of dishes to put in the tub.

FEIGA

Please, Sonia, tonight you don't need to work . . . You
should be out there with Mendel and the baby.

SONIA

It's okay – such a wonderful meal – I have to do something.
You have such a beautiful home.

FEIGA

Bless God. The kids are healthy, they have what to eat – that's
what's important.

*Sonia hands Feiga the last of the dishes she's holding, then she leaves
the kitchen . . .*

INT. SENDER'S APARTMENT. DINING-ROOM – NIGHT

*Sender is sitting alone at the dinner table. Sonia collects a few more
dishes, then:*

SENDER

Have a second?

*Sonia stops, surprised. Sender reaches into his pocket, and pulls out a
jewel-encrusted brooch. He holds it out. Sonia hesitates, looking into the
next room.*

*Sonia's POV – Mendel, holding their son, is involved in an animated
conversation with his brother-in-law Schmuel.*

Relax, it's not for you. I just want your opinion.

*Sonia puts down the dishes and takes the brooch from Sender's hand. A
green stone set in a delicately cast gold backing.*

My principal buyer came across it. It's an antique brooch
from Paris, circa 1880, from Querelle. That's a single carat
emerald set in gold. My wife's birthday is coming up, so I
thought I'd surprise her.

SONIA

It's beautiful.

SENDER

Five thousand bucks. What a bargain, huh?

Sonia forces a smile, and hands back the brooch.

SONIA

You did great.

SENDER

Bullshit.

Sonia's jaw drops.

I understand your father, may his memory be a blessing, was
the finest gemologist in New Jersey.
(*Sonia is speechless*)
I also understand that you picked up a thing or two from him.

*He holds out the brooch. Cheeks burning, Sonia takes it from him again
and gives it a quick look-over.*

SONIA

Querelle never designed a base like this. I can't tell what the
date on it is, but it isn't 1880. I also think if you check on this
emerald you'll find it's probably a composite – maybe just a
layer of emerald fused into glass and backed by foil to give it
all that brilliance. It's excellent work, but I wouldn't price it
at a dime over eight hundred bucks.

Sender's eyes sparkle.

SENDER

Why didn't you go into the business?

SONIA

My parents didn't want me mixing with . . . unsavory
characters.
(*shooting Sender a quick look*)
They wanted me to marry a great scholar and live a decent,
spiritual Jewish life.

SENDER

Did you?

Sonia is silent, confused.

34

Did you marry a great scholar?

SONIA

That, I'm not qualified to answer. But I know I married a *tzaddik*.

SENDER .

A holy man? Don't you think our Mendel's a little young for such distinction?

SONIA

Age has nothing to do with it. You're either born with the heart of a *tzaddik*, or you're not.

SENDER

And your heart?

Again Sonia is stunned into silence. Sender leans closer to her.

Is it in your heart to be the wife of a *tzaddik*?

Sonia's lip trembles . . . sweat beads on her brow, as Mendel's eyes bore into her, then:

RACHEL
(*off-screen*)

All right, dessert's on the table!

Feiga bustles into the dining-room, followed by a flock of eager children.

Sonia is in shock. Sender reaches out and takes the brooch from her hand, then he's assaulted by his youngest son, who jumps up into his lap . . . Sender laughs merrily, lifting the boy up into the air.

CUT TO:

Cold water splashing from the faucet, into Sonia's hands . . . She is bent over the sink in the kitchen, splashing her face with the cold water.

RACHEL

Sonia?

Sonia straightens up, dripping water. Her face is flushed.

Gottenyu, you're red as a beet.

She puts her hands on Sonia's cheeks.

And hot like an oven. You're burning with fever, poor thing, why didn't you say something?

Sonia tries to talk, but her breath just comes out in short gasps.

INT. SENDER'S APARTMENT. BEDROOM – NIGHT

Rachel leads Sonia into the dark room, leaving the door partially open to allow in the light from the hallway. Sonia is gulping in air like a woman who has been drowning.

RACHEL

Sit . . . sit on the bed, you're having a panic attack. Breathe slowly . . . breathe . . .

She sits on the bed beside Sonia, massaging her arms and neck.

Your muscles are like iron knots . . . breathe . . . just relax and breathe. It must be overwhelming for you – a new city, a new family, all these new pressures . . .

Sonia begins to relax under Rachel's ministrations, her head slightly tilting back.

You're just wound up too tight . . . Just relax and breathe . . . Relax . . .

And then, somehow, Sonia's face is right beside Rachel's . . . Her mouth opens and she embraces her sister-in-law with a real kiss on the lips. It holds for a brief instant, then Rachel pushes her away.

My God.
(*shaking her head*)
Sonia . . . what's gotten into you?

Sonia is as shocked by her actions as Rachel is . . . She raises her hands to cover her trembling mouth.

You need help.

CUT TO:

INT. REBBE'S HOME. OFFICE – DAY

A door swings open revealing a warm, spacious room cluttered with

books. The Hassidic Rebbe Moishe Shimeon Myerson sits behind a
cluttered desk. He is surrounded by several of his gabbaim – a kind of
personal guard composed of his most devoted disciples. They lean close to
the Rebbe as he speaks in a low voice – straining to catch his every
word.

Sonia is standing in the open doorway, trembling with nervousness. She
looks back over her shoulder.

Rachel is sitting in the waiting-room behind her, among a group of
Women waiting their turn for an audience with the Rebbe. She makes a
'Go on!' gesture with her hands.

VOICE
(off-screen)

You can see the Rebbe now.

A Young Gabbai is standing beside Sonia. She swallows hard.

SONIA

I . . . some of these other people have been waiting longer . . .
I think another day might be . . .

She starts to beat a retreat, but Rachel intercepts her and pushes her
back through the doorway . . .

37

RACHEL

(*whispering*)

Don't make a scene.

Rachel then backs away, leaving Sonia standing alone in the doorway. Sonia raises her eyes.

The Rebbe and all his gabbaim are looking at her curiously.

REBBE

Come on in, Mrs Horowitz.

Sonia bites her lip and eyes on the floor. She steps forward until she is in front of the Rebbe's desk. The Rebbe whispers a few words to his gabbaim, and all but one of them turn and file out of the room. The remaining gabbai gestures to Sonia:

GABBAI

Take a seat.

As Sonia sits down the Rebbitzn – the Rebbe's stern-looking, stately wife – enters from the kitchen and pours some tea into her husband's cup, then glides back out of the room.

The Rebbe's voice is so soft it takes a moment for Sonia to realize she is being spoken to.

REBBE

I understand your husband is a truly inspired teacher as well as a great scholar. Filling the hearts of our children with a love of Toyre is the greatest *mitzvah* of all, in God's eyes.

Sonia tries to force a smile – but it comes off looking more sickly than anything.

The Rebbe studies her with clear, piercing eyes.

Most people are practically falling over themselves to get in here – but you look like you'd give up your firstborn just to get out.

Sonia tries to say something, but she can't manage a sound. She looks at the Rebbe . . . then at the gabbai standing beside him. Then back at the floor.

REBBE

He's making you nervous?

Sonia stays silent. The Rebbe sighs, then whispers a few words to his gabbai, who turns and steps into the kitchen. A moment later the Rebbitzn enters the room, and stands by the wall, behind her husband.

Sonia looks up at the Rebbitzn, but the old woman makes no attempt to acknowledge her.

I understand you're troubled.

SONIA

I . . . I'm not sure what I'm supposed to . . .
        (shakes her head)
I can't find the words.

REBBE

The Almighty gave you a soul to nurture. He gave you a body in which to house it. He gave you a mind in order to understand your soul's needs, and he gave you a tongue in order to express them. If the desire to heal your soul is strong enough, you'll find the words.

SONIA

I'm not even sure . . . where my body ends and my soul begins.

A moment of silence. Then Sonia speaks haltingly:

I feel . . . ever since I was, I don't know, a very young girl . . . I felt, I feel like there's a fire, a warm fire somewhere inside of me. It used to be nice – it kept me warm – but it's been getting hotter and hotter . . . I feel it growing inside me. It makes my stomach burn . . . my nerves, my skin . . .

The Rebbe looks down at his desk, unable to completely hide his discomfort at the direction Sonia's discourse is taking. The Rebbitzn keeps her eyes focused somewhere on the far wall, but her jaw is tight.

. . . my skin is so hot . . . it's so sensitive now, I can hardly put on a shirt without . . . I can't even nurse my child for the intensity of the . . . I . . .

(pausing for breath)
It's too hot. Everything is too hot. Every touch burns me.
(tears glitter in her eyes)
I have no soul. I have no soul, and without a soul my body is consuming itself like a house on fire.

The Rebbe's face is slightly red. He unconsciously dabs at his cheek with his sleeve.

REBBE

The Almighty gave every one of us a soul. Whatever torment you are suffering, you must always remember that. You have a soul.

SONIA

Maybe. But if I do . . .
(looks directly at the Rebbe)
It wasn't God that gave it to me.

CLOSE ON: *the Rebbe, his lips trembling slightly, as we dissolve the setting sun into the frame – seemingly burning his image away until only the sun remains.*

The sun descends in fast-motion, and we tilt down with it as it sets behind the Brooklyn skyline, plunging the city into darkness.

INT. REBBE'S HOME. OFFICE – NIGHT

The Rebbe is still at his desk, once again surrounded by his gabbaim. The room is illuminated by bright electric lamps. One Young Gabbai is reading from a newspaper:

YOUNG GABBAI

– And so, once again, by supporting the Godless state of Israel, in defiance of biblical prophesy and the holy redemption of the Jewish people through God's grace alone – Boro Park's Rebbe Moishe Myerson has demonstrated that he is little more than a gentile heretic in the guise of a Jew.

The other young men react with an explosion of angry remonstrations.

40

GABBAI #2

Who do these people think they are? They've gone too far this
time, these fanatics . . .

*But the Rebbe isn't really paying attention to all this. He is staring past
them into the next room:*

*Rebbe's POV of the kitchen, where, through the half-open door, his wife
is visible, moving around the stove, preparing dinner. She reaches for
something up in the cupboard, and the kerchief covering her grey hair
comes loose and floats to the floor . . . She bends down to pick it up.*

GABBAI #3
(*off-screen*)

Rebbe, please tell us you're not going to let this attack go
without a stinging rebuttal . . .

CLOSE ON: *The Rebbe watching his wife intently, a spark lighting in
his eyes . . .*

GABBAI #2
(*off-screen*)

Rebbe? If you prefer, we can compose a letter and you
can . . .

REBBE

Tomorrow.

GABBAI #1
(*off-screen*)

But . . . but Rebbe, by tomorrow this article will be all over
the . . .

REBBE

I said *tomorrow.*

*The gabbaim all fall silent. They look at their Rebbe in surprise, then
quickly nod and begin collecting their things and filing out of the room,
wishing the Rebbe 'Good night' as they step out through the doorway.*

INT. REBBE'S HOME. KITCHEN – NIGHT

*The Rebbitzn is mixing the stew in a large pot on the stove, when a pair
of hands reach in and clamp over her eyes. She gives a shriek and drops*

her ladle into the pot. The Rebbe then leans into the frame and whispers in her ear:

                    REBBE
Guess who?

The Rebbitzn turns around, her nose practically touching her husband's.

                    REBBITZN
Have you gone crazy? You could give a person a heart attack.

                    REBBE
Something smells good.

                    REBBITZN
It's the *chulent*. I'm making it special, for . . .

                    REBBE
No, that's not it . . .

He leans closer to his stunned wife, sniffing her cheek and neck . . .

It's you that smells so good.

He takes her face in his hands.

God forgive me, but I think it's twenty years since I told you how beautiful you look.

                    REBBITZN
It's been twenty years since I looked beautiful.

The Rebbe kisses her full on the mouth. She gasps . . .

Moish! You've heard too many evil stories today.

                    REBBE
Sometimes it's the exposure to evil that brings out our best sides.

He pulls his wife closer.

                    REBBITZN
You shouldn't get so excited, Moish. The doctor said you can't allow yourself to get . . .

REBBE

The doctor? What does a doctor know about love?

He gives his wife a gentle, romantic kiss – He smiles at her then pulls her to him and embraces her even more powerfully than before.

CUT TO:

A Hassidic man howling like a banshee – grabbing the lapel of his jacket and tearing it right down the middle . . . Pull back to reveal:

The entire street clogged with black-clad Hassidim – weeping, wailing, gnashing their teeth in a genuine show of unadulterated grief. We dolly past their anguished faces, then boom up over the sea of black hats:

A podium has been erected on the front steps of the main synagogue. Behind the microphone, the Rebbe's Chief Gabbai is delivering a heartfelt eulogy in a voice cracking with emotion.

CHIEF GABBAI

– When the Rebbe's heart stopped beating last night, we lost more than just a man – for his was a heart that beat not only to maintain the life of one man; it beat to maintain the vital circulation of the entire nation of Yisroel. And who can even begin to understand what force could be strong enough to still such a heart?

ANGLE ON: *Sonia standing beside Rachel amidst the women gathered around the outskirts of the throng of men. Both women are holding on to strollers bearing their babies. Dolly in on Sonia's face, as the gabbai continues:*

– What kind of a terrible power could have caused such a tragedy?

The crowd near Sonia parts . . . and an entourage of mourning Women, flanking the Rebbitzn, make their way past. It seems that they are going to continue on their way, but the Rebbitzn stops.

The Rebbitzn pauses for a moment, then turns and steps in front of Sonia. She stares at her with hard, grey eyes. Sonia is utterly confounded. The crowd around them is hushed . . . also unsure of what is transpiring.

The Rebbitzn cranes her neck forward, so that her lips are right beside Sonia's ear, and whispers something that only Sonia can hear. Then the Rebbitzn moves away, and Sonia is left standing there, stricken.

RACHEL
(*under her breath*)
Sonia? What did she say? Sonia?

Then there is the sound of an awful cackle:

The Beggar Woman is standing among the crowd of women, her bright rags a jolt of rude color against the sea of mourners' black. She is laughing, looking right at Sonia.

Sonia suddenly turns and bolts, pushing her stroller ahead of her, parting the crowd as if it was the Red Sea.

INT. HOROWITZ APARTMENT – DAY

Sonia pushes the stroller in and slams the door shut behind herself; she pauses for breath . . . but now Shimmie is crying urgently.

Sonia lifts him up out of the stroller and bounces him against her breast.

SONIA
There, there, *tataleh* . . . shhh . . . it's all right . . .

But the baby won't stop crying. Sonia removes the bottle from the stroller and tries to feed it to her child, but he turns his head away, wailing even more insistently.

Sonia snaps. She puts the crying baby back in the stroller then runs out of the living-room.

INT. BEDROOM – DAY

Sonia bursts in, slides to her knees on the floor and, like a little girl, pulls the blanket off the bed and covers herself with it.

Under the blanket, which we can somehow see under, Sonia covers her ears with her hands, trying to shut out the world . . . but:

VOICE
(*off-screen*)
Why are you hiding?

Sonia's eyes look to her side, where, under the blanket beside her, her brother Yossi is sitting.

45

YOSSI

There's no one here but you. Who are you hiding from?

Sonia just claps her hands over her ears and squeezes her eyes shut. But now an insistent buzzing is intruding on the silence. Sonia ignores it, but the buzzing continues . . . and finally she is forced to open her eyes.

CUT TO:

The blackness opening up accompanied by the sound of a creaking door, revealing Sender Horowitz's bearded face . . .

SENDER

Are you . . . cold?

REVERSE ON: *Sonia – standing behind the door, still holding the blanket wrapped around her. The baby is crying in the background.*

SONIA

Mendel isn't home.

SENDER

I know. Can I come in?

Sonia steps back, allowing Sender into the living-room. Sender leans over the baby carriage where little Shimmie is bawling. He gently touches a finger to the baby's lips, and whispers:

Shh.

The baby is instantly silent. Sender straightens up and looks at Sonia.

Actually, it was you I came for.

Sonia stands silently in the middle of the room, wrapped up in her blanket.

I want to offer you a job.

Sonia blinks, confused.

Your analysis of the brooch I showed you last shabbes was spot on. I'd like you to run my store here in Boro Park.

SONIA

I thought you worked in Manhattan. I didn't know you had a store in the neighborhood.

46

That's because I don't . . .

(he smiles)

At least not officially. It's a basement in an apartment only a few blocks away. From there I sell a select variety of jewelry – only the very finest pieces. Customers from all over the world come here to buy, because they know by me they're getting only the best.

Sender slowly circles around Sonia, moving in closer.

My buyer, Heschel, has – had – impeccable taste. But he's getting old. There doesn't exist a glasses prescription strong enough to help his eyes anymore. I want you to take over for him. I'll introduce you to all my suppliers – you'll go into the city three days a week and pick out only the best pieces you come across. There should be no more than thirty or forty pieces in the store at any given time – each one something Queen Elizabeth would feel comfortable wearing if somebody made off with her family jewels. Three days a week you stay in the store to sell. But the other three you'll be in the city, on 47th Street, all over – sometimes even out of state for a few days on a special buy. So . . .

(stops circling)

What do you say?

Sonia is dumbfounded. But she manages to croak out:

SONIA

I'm . . . a mother now.

SENDER

Half the mothers in Boro Park are running cash businesses out of their own basements. The days that you're in the city you can leave Shimmie by my wife, or by Rachel. The other days you keep him with you in the store.

SONIA

Does Mendel . . . approve of this?

SENDER

Does it matter?

Sonia's eyes narrow.

> SONIA
>
> Does he even know about it?

> SENDER
>
> I thought I'd let you tell him.

> SONIA
>
> I may be a little out of my depth right now . . . but I'm not a
> fool. A cash business means no taxes paid. And no taxes paid
> means theft. Even if it's from the government – it's a sin.

Sender regards Sonia closely.

> SENDER
>
> Once . . . when I was a boy, I stole the answers to a test from
> my teacher's drawer. I copied them, and put them back
> before he noticed. I got a hundred on the test, and I felt
> terrific. I was dancing for a week, like Gene Kelly.
> > (*pause*)
>
> I knew then that my own conscience would be useless to me
> in preventing further transgressions. So without telling him
> why, I asked my father to teach me how to avoid sin. He told
> me about his teacher in Lubin, a *tzaddik* who kept a notebook
> in which he recorded all his sins – from the day of his bar
> mitzvah onward. One day, when he was ninety-three years
> old, the *tzaddik* forgot his notebook on his desk in the
> Yeshiva. Just one notebook – most people would have a
> library full. My father and some of the other boys ran over to
> see what sins the great rebbe had committed. But when they
> opened the notebook, they couldn't believe their eyes – the
> first page had not yet even been completely filled up.

*Sender is very close to Sonia. He reaches over and gently removes the
blanket from her shoulders.*

> If we all wrote down our sins, my father said, we'd be more
> careful about committing them. We sin because we're
> careless, and we don't think about it.

*Sener lays the blanket over a chair, and steps back toward Sonia, whose
every muscle is trembling with vulnerability.*

But there was something that bothered me about that story. See, even if the *tzaddik* was very old, if he had enough presence of mind to keep recording his sins, how could he be so careless as to leave the evidence lying around for everyone to find? And it was then, only then, that I understood . . .

Sender takes Sonia's hand in his. She flushes, but she doesn't move.

It was a front. He kept the book of sins for his students to discover – but his other sins, he kept in his heart, for they were dearer to him even than was God, and he couldn't bear to part with them. Because in a world where piety is the standard by which we are judged . . .

His other hand reaches up and caresses the back of Sonia's neck.

It's the quality of our sins that sets us apart.

He kisses Sonia's neck. She tries to push him back, but he's too forceful, and she's too overwhelmed to resist. She begins to return his embrace and, as her arms close around him, Sender moves her back to the wall, crushing her with his body, making her gasp. He hikes up her dress.

CLOSE ON: *Sonia's face, her cheek pressed against the wall . . . There is the sound of Sender's zipper being opened and then his face is beside Sonia's. She gasps. Sender thrusts heavily several times, his breathing is heavy – Sonia's face is flushed in a mixture of shock and pleasure. Then, as quickly as it happened, it is over. Off-screen the baby is crying again. Sender raises the 'Querelle' brooch into the frame near Sonia's eyes. He holds it there and whispers in her ear:*

You'll start on Monday.

Sonia's hand closes over the brooch – and Sender is gone from the frame. We hold on Sonia, as she hears the sound of Sender's retreating footsteps, the door opening and closing, leaving her alone with the sound of her wailing child.

FADE TO BLACK

In the darkness the baby's cries blend into the wail of a siren, and we open on:

EXT. 47TH STREET. DIAMOND DISTRICT – DAY

Sonia walking up the bustling sidewalk, passing store windows filled with mountainous displays of jewelry . . . She brushes past Pakistani 'hawkers' standing outside the doors of their stores, trying to lure in customers, past speeding messengers, past Hassidic men walking in pairs . . . A slight smile begins twinkling in her eyes, as the camera booms up, looking down on the busy street as Sonia mingles with the crowd.

INT. 'TOP NOTCH' JEWELRY STORE – DAY

EXTREME CLOSE-UP: *on a pair of hands, carefully swabbing a bright ring. There is the sound of a bell and we rack focus to:*

Sonia as she steps into the store and walks up to the counter, where she is met by the Man – his back is still toward us – who was cleaning the ring.

> SONIA
> Good morning, Mr Kapoor. I'm Sonia Horowitz – Sender Horowitz's new buyer.

REVERSE ANGLE: *on a young Hispanic Man with deep green eyes. He shifts nervously.*

> YOUNG MAN
> Uh, good morning, Miss Horowitz. But I'm not . . .

> SONIA
> Actually, It's *Mrs* Horowitz. And there's something I'd like to show you.

She holds up the fake 'Querelle' brooch.

> Recognize this?

The Young Man shakes his head, trying to speak, but:

> No? You can't remember an antique brooch designed by Querelle that's worth thirty thousand bucks – which you parted with for five, but is really worth nothing because it's a fake, is that what you can't remember?

> YOUNG MAN
> I . . . can hardly remember my own name, at this point . . .

Hrundi Kapoor, a middle-aged Indian man, steps up to the Young Man's side:

KAPOOR

Ramon.

(to Sonia)

I'm Hrundi Kapoor.

Sonia stands there, her momentum completely broken.

RAMON

I just work here . . . this is, uh . . .

He backs off, scratching his head, as Kapoor indicates the brooch in Sonia's hand.

KAPOOR

I've never seen that piece before.

Sonia recovers, overcoming her flustered insecurity with an intense bravado.

SONIA

You should be ashamed of yourself, Mr Kapoor. Mr Horowitz's previous buyer may have been too old, or maybe just too trusting to detect this fake, but he can remember who he bought it from.

Kapoor starts to protest, but Sonia cuts him off.

We have two possibilities here, Mr Kapoor: One, you yourself didn't know it was a fake and unwittingly passed it on. Two, you knew. Either way you're doing dishonorable business. As I understand it, if Mr Horowitz so desired, he could tarnish your reputation so thoroughly that within a week you'd be out on the street hawking watches out of a suitcase.

Kapoor grits his teeth. He's sweating.

Normally Mr Horowitz would have come down and told you all this himself – but I think he was a little concerned about losing his temper. So here I am. And though I happen to have a temper myself, I have no particular emotional investment in this unfortunate transaction – so it might be possible for you

and I to start over on a fresh page and embark on a
relationship that will better profit both yourself and Mr
Horowitz. The emphasis, of course, being on Mr Horowitz.
                         (*pause*)
What do you say, Mr Kapoor?

*Kapoor is stuck. He shoots an angry look over at Ramon, who is
standing there, watching like a spectator. Ramon instantly drops his
eyes.*

Kapoor turns back to Sonia, face tight.

                         KAPOOR
What can I say?

                         SONIA
How about: Good morning, Mrs Horowitz, welcome to 47th
Street. From now on I'll be selling to you at 80 percent below
retail. Is there anything I can interest you in today?

Kappor can hardly gather his wits. He grimaces slightly, then:

                         KAPOOR
Good morning, Mrs Horowitz . . . welcome to 47th Street.

CUT TO:

INT. BORO PARK. BASEMENT 'STORE' – DAY

*Sender is introducing Sonia to a wealthy Israeli Couple, whose backs
are toward the camera.*

                         SENDER
Mr Mizrachi, Mrs Mizrachi – Mrs Horowitz is my new buyer.
I'm sure Heschel will be missed, but I promise you whatever
she might lack in experience, Mrs Horowitz more than makes
up for with her superb taste.

The couple nod at Sonia. We hear the man say, 'I'm sure she will.'

                         ISRAELI WOMAN
Any relations?

SONIA
(*stunned*)
Excuse me?

SENDER
(*stepping in, with a laugh*)
She's my sister-in-law, Mrs Mizrachi. I'm keeping things in
the family, so she can put my brother through Yeshiva.

CUT TO:

*A mirror being turned revealing the face of a wealthy-looking Woman
in a dark suit. She touches the pearl earrings hanging from her ears.
Sonia leans into the frame.*

SONIA
You like them, Mrs Gelbart?

MRS GELBART
What I would *like* is for my husband, God bless him, to get
off his fat ass and surprise me with something, instead of
handing me a wad of cash and telling me to go make myself
happy.

SONIA
I understand, Mrs Gelbart, but the joy of the surprise lasts
only a few moments, and you're at the mercy of his taste. At
least this way you can choose a piece that will give you *naches*
for the rest of your life . . .

CUT TO:

*Sonia, bouncing her son in her arms, sitting at a teakwood desk across
from a sharply dressed Young Man. A display of rings is on the desk
top. The man picks up a sleekly designed ring.*

SONIA
You have excellent taste, Mr Sugarman. That ring was
designed by Eddie Sakamoto. You've got a beautiful
combination of cabochon and faceted gemstones laid in a
platinum band. That design won the first prize in the
'Spectrum' competition last fall.

54

MR SUGARMAN

What, ah, range are we talking about here?

SONIA

I'm not going to pretend I'm gonna give you some kind of
fancy bargain, Mr Sugarman – I'll sell it to you for what it's
worth, but that in itself is a bargain, considering the quality of
the piece and limited availability of this design.

CUT TO:

EXT. FRONT STOOP. STORE – DAY

*Mr Sugarman leaves the building, nodding at Nelson – the store's
'security' – a burly black man who is standing out on the steps, keeping
an eye on the street.*

INT. BASEMENT 'STORE' – DAY

*A wall safe swings open. Sonia reaches in, deposits a tremendous wad of
cash and closes the safe again.*

CUT TO:

A middle-aged man, wearing the small yarmulke *of the modern
orthodox, sits across the desk from Sonia. His name is Mr Fishbein, and
he grins what only his mother could think is a charming grin.*

MR FISHBEIN

It's so nice to see a new face here. Very inspirational. It just
makes me want to . . . *buy* something.

He winks.

SONIA

Since it's your wife's birthday, Mr Fishbein, I'd recommend
this silver bracelet inlaid with ruby. It's her birthstone, as it is
mine. It should make a lovely . . .

MR FISHBEIN

Could you model it for me?

Sonia smiles tightly and slips on the bracelet.

55

It looks fabulous – but I imagine on such a lovely wrist anything would.

SONIA

The question is whether or not you think your wife, Mrs Fishbein, will like it.

Fishbein takes Sonia's hand in his own, removing the bracelet from her wrist.

MR FISHBEIN

The question is, Mrs Horowitz, why a woman as lovely as you are isn't wearing any jewelry of her own.

He grins his loopy grin, as Sonia gently extracts his hand from around hers.

CUT TO:

INT. HOROWITZ APARTMENT. KITCHEN – NIGHT

The door of a microwave oven is opened, and a kosher dinner is shoved into it. Sonia shuts it, sets the timer and turns back into the kitchen. Mendel is sitting at the table, the baby beside him in a high-chair.

Sonia picks up the baby's bottle and tries to feed it to him, but he turns his head away.

MENDEL

So . . . you've stopped, uh, breast-feeding Shimmie?

Sonia shrugs, continuing her fruitless efforts to feed the baby.

Isn't it a little soon?

SONIA

Soon for what?

MENDEL

I understand it's supposed to be, you know . . . important, for a child to be naturally fed for at least three months in order to develop healthy parental bonding.

SONIA

'Healthy parental bonding?'

Mendel gently takes the bottle from Sonia's frustrated fingers and feeds it to Shimmie, who accepts it from him.

MENDEL

I read it in an article.

SONIA

Between all your teaching and all your learning you found time to read articles, now?

The timer beeps. Sonia walks over to the microwave, pops it open and pulls out Mendel's dinner. She puts it down in front of him, then sits across from him. Mendel closes his eyes and silently mouths a prayer. Sonia stares at him with irritation. He opens his eyes, and digs into his meal, chewing silently.

Well?

Mendel looks up.

Well?

MENDEL

It's good.

Mendel continues eating.

SONIA

But what?

MENDEL

But nothing. It's good. I didn't say but.

SONIA

But you thought it. I could see it in the air like a little grey cloud. A little cloudy 'but' something. *But what?*

MENDEL

I understand that most of the nutrients you can find in freshly cooked foods are absent in microwaveable products.

SONIA

It sounds to me like you've been reading articles on a rather wide variety of subjects. Or, more likely, you've been getting an earful from your sister Rachel – in which case I'd thank her to keep her nose out of my affairs.

*Mendel looks up sharply. Sonia stops. Did she say the wrong word?
Mendel puts down his fork and looks at her.*

Do you know what today is, Mendel?

Mendel shakes his head.

It's my birthday.

Mendel's spirits sag. He knows he's blown it.

MENDEL

Sonia . . .

*He reaches out to take her hand, but she draws it away. Mendel is
stricken. He speaks softly.*

I know you're working now and I know you enjoy it. So I'm
glad for you. But you run out of the house at the crack of
dawn – I hardly ever see you and when I do it's to get a
microwave dinner tossed at me like I'm some kind of charity
case. Now, I know I spend my day with my nose stuck in a
book, but I'm not a complete idiot when it comes to these
things. You say you're happy – but it's clear that something's
missing. What is it, Sonia?

SONIA

What is *what?*

MENDEL

What is it that you want?

SONIA

I don't *know*, Mendel . . . if I knew . . .

She looks up at her husband.

I just want something beautiful.

MENDEL

But you have it, Sonia. You have it right here. A home, a
child and a husband who loves you more than anything in the
world.

SONIA

In this world, maybe . . .

She draws closer to Mendel – her voice is desperate.

But what about the other world, Mendel? The world of the spirit? The world of the Toyre and the Talmud and the Holy of Holies? Do you love me more than that, too? What about God, Mendel . . .?

Mendel has tears in his eyes . . . he can't meet Sonia's erupting passion, and just shakes his head in confusion.

Do you love me more than you love God?

MENDEL

Sonia . . . that's a terrible thing to ask.

Sonia moves away from Mendel.

SONIA

I'm sorry, Mendel. You're a good man. And this life is good. But it's not beautiful.

MENDEL

Goodness *is* beauty.

SONIA

No. Beauty has goodness in it – but it can also be terrible.

MENDEL

Is that what you want? That things should be terrible . . .?

Tears stream down from Mendel's tormented eyes.

Is that what should make you happy?

CUT TO:

INT. BASEMENT 'STORE' – DAY

CLOSE ON: *Sonia in a position that looks as if her back is against the wall. Her cheeks are flushed and we can see that Sender is pressed against her, face buried in her neck, grunting as he pushes into her. We pull back and revolve the camera, revealing that Sonia is lying on the teakwood desk, with Sender lying heavily on top of her. Her skirt is lifted up, but she is otherwise completely dressed. Her fingers dig into Sender's shirt-covered back, as their movements grow faster, breath shorter . . .*

EXT. FRONT STOOP. 'STORE' – DAY

Nelson stops a customer on the steps outside, indicating his watch . . . He apologizes for the inconvenience as the customer reluctantly leaves.

INT. BASEMENT 'STORE' – DAY

It's over. Sender immediately begins to rise, but Sonia's hands, almost involuntarily, hold him fast.

> SONIA

Stay . . .

Sender looks questioningly into her eyes, which she averts in shame.

. . . just for a moment. Stay.

Sender runs his finger over Sonia's exposed ear and whispers.

> SENDER

In heaven there is a catalogue of sins as vast as the clouds; but here and now the only true sin is weakness . . .

Sonia touches her fingers to Sender's lips.

> SONIA

Don't.

Sender moves her hand aside with his own and leans closer to her.

> SENDER

A woman of fortitude, who can find? For her price is far above rubies. When her husband relies on her, he shall lack no fortune. She arises while it's dark to feed her household. Strength and majesty are her raiment; and joyfully she can anticipate the day of judgement.

Sonia's eyes glitter with tears, as Sender continues:

False is grandeur and vain is beauty. Only a God-fearing woman deserves praise; give her the fruits of her handiwork

and let her be praised at the gates of heaven for her countless deeds.

The tears stream down Sonia's cheeks, as she gazes into the distance.

SONIA

Sometimes I look at men and think – How can this be? How can God have created so ugly a creature for woman to cling to? Is it some kind of an awful test . . . or is it just a joke? Men are ugly . . . but you, Sender Horowitz . . .

She turns and faces Sender, her eyes looking into his.

You are the ugliest man of all.

Sender leans down, kissing Sonia full on the mouth and the image begins to blur and lose focus, blending into that of:

A blur of sparkling light, which comes into sharp focus as the glittering surface of a diamond.

VOICE
(*off-screen*)

It's a flawless brilliant-cut stone from South Africa. Top of the line . . .

Sonia is standing across the counter from Hrundi Kapoor, appraising the stone set in a classic Tiffany-style ring, looking at it through a loupe *– a jeweller's magnifying glass.*

SONIA

Hm. How's business, Mr Kapoor?

KAPOOR

Business? The rich are buying at Tiffany's and Saks. The poor people are carjacking the rich ones and everybody else is sitting on their couch and watching the Home Shopping Network.

SONIA

Not surprising, if this is the kind of merchandise you're showcasing.

A chuckle off-screen – Kapoor turns and shoots an irritated look at:

Ramon, who is standing nearby, arranging a display of earrings. Ramon bites his lip; goes on with his work.

KAPOOR

Listen here, Mrs Horowitz. I triple-check everything I show you. That's a perfectly sound diamond in a perfectly sound ring.

SONIA

It's perfectly sound and perfectly boring.

She puts it on the counter and slides it over to where Ramon is working.

Back me up here.

Ramon blinks; he does not want to be caught in the middle of this.

Boring or not?

Ramon looks up at Sonia. She won't relent. He gives a resigned shrug.

RAMON

Boring.

KAPOOR

Ramon – isn't today your *–* ?

RAMON

Half day – today I'm outta here at . . .
(*looks at his watch*)
Now. I'm outta here now. Thanks, Mr Kapoor . . .

He eases his way out, as Kapoor steps in front of Sonia again.

KAPOOR

It's a classic, Mrs Horowitz. The point of a classic is its
steadfastness. There are some things nobody wants to change.
I was holding it just for you – but I'll be more than happy to
show it to . . .

He reaches for the ring, but her hand closes over it first.

SONIA

No, no . . . I'll take it.
(*sighs*)
The sad fact is, it's probably the best piece I've seen all week.
Lucky me, that it's on an 80 percent discount rate.

Kapoor purses his lips, and reaches for some forms.

KAPOOR

Good choice, Mrs Horowitz.

*Sonia watches Ramon hurry out of the shop, fumbling as he pulls on his
jacket as he goes. Then:*

VOICE
(*off-screen*)

I like this one.

*Sonia turns. Her brother Yossi is standing beside her, looking at a small
pile of gold jewelry on the counter.*

SONIA

Since when are *you* an expert?

Kapoor looks up at Sonia.

KAPOOR

Excuse me?

YOSSI

I didn't say I was an expert. I just like this one.

SONIA

Which one?

YOSSI

That one.

Kapoor is pointing to a gold ring in the pile.

KAPOOR

This one?

SONIA

Can I see it, please?

Kapoor nods, looking at Sonia like she's crazy, as she picks the ring up. It's intricately designed. She puts the loupe *to her eye and closely examines it:*

The ring is carved in the shape of two figures – one a man and the other a woman, wrapped around each other, their hands outstretched to hold the empty mount where a stone is supposed to go.

What is this?

KAPOOR

Just some free-floating junk that came in with a batch of useless gold items. I sell them to the melter's at cost.

SONIA

Where is this one from?

KAPOOR

Somewhere, Chinatown, I don't know.

Sonia looks at Kapoor.

SONIA

Chinatown? I am holding the most . . .
                    (*shaking her head*)
You look at a piece like this, call it a piece of junk from Chinatown, and you wonder why business is bad?

KAPOOR

What, did God put you on this earth for the sole purpose of busting my chops? If you like it, I'll throw it in with the other one, all right?

Sonia fixes Kapoor with a steely gaze . . . then smiles slightly.

SONIA

All right. But you tell me where you got that ring.

CUT TO:

INT. DIAMOND EXCHANGE - DAY

A light 'Klezmer' melody begins on the soundtrack, as Sonia walks past counters filled with all manner of sparkling jewelry . . . until she is in front of a counter where a young Satmar Hassid is working.

SATMAR HASSID

Good morning, Mrs Horowitz, how are you?

SONIA

Baruch Hashem.

She puts the gold ring down on the counter.

Do you have any idea who might have manufactured this ring?

The Satmar Hassid picks it up, turning it over in his delicate fingers.

SATMAR HASSID

It's missing a stone.

Sonia raises her eyebrows: 'Obviously.'

The Hassid raises a loupe *to his eye and inspects the ring more closely.*

It isn't marked . . . doesn't look like the work of any designer I'm familiar with . . . maybe some kind of *chachka* from Chinatown?

Sonia's jaw clenches. She reaches over and plucks the ring right out of the young Hassid's surprised fingers.

CUT TO:

A STREET SIGN: 'CANAL STREET – CHINATOWN'

The camera booms down to the incredibly crowded, noisy sidewalk, stopping on Sonia's face. She looks around herself, grits her teeth, and steps up to the display window of a local jewelry store. It's filled with all manner of thick, gaudy, hideous gold jewelry.

Sonia wrinkles her nose in distaste, but she steels herself and enters the shop.

CUT TO:

A CHINATOWN 'MONTAGE'

Sonia questions a number of Chinese jewelry merchants, who brusquely look over her ring and shake their heads.

Images of the bustling activity as Sonia wanders into the streets . . . vendors selling strange-looking seafood . . . packs of running children . . . ducks and spare ribs hanging in restaurant windows . . .

Sonia's gaze is fixed by the steaming stand of an outdoor food vendor . . . Sonia's POV slowly zooms in and the entire screen is engulfed in white steam.

CUT TO:

EXT. BENNET PARK – DAY

The steam clears, and a wide angle shows Sonia sitting alone on a bench, munching on an egg roll.

> YOSSI'S VOICE
> You're going to hell.

A closer shot shows Sonia and Yossi sitting side by side.

> SONIA
> For eating an egg roll?

> YOSSI
> For eating pig.

> SONIA
> It's delicious.

66

You're going to hell.

Really? And yesterday, when I was lying on a desk, getting schtupped by my brother-in-law – yesterday I wasn't going to hell?

Yossi clamps his hands over his ears and hums. Sonia's expression sinks.

Oh, I'm sorry . . . Yossi, come on, I'm sorry. I'll shut up, okay?

VOICE
(*off-screen*)

Little boys always hate any noise they aren't making themselves.

The old Beggar Woman from Boro Park is standing in front of them, leaning on a shopping cart filled with bric-à-brac. She reaches out and caresses Yossi's head, then takes a chocolate bar out of her coat pocket and holds it out to him.

OLD WOMAN

Something sweet with which to coat the world's bitter pill, *tataleh*.

Yossi takes the chocolate bar. A Passerby bumps into the Old Woman. He apologizes, reaches into his pocket and hands her a few coins before continuing on his way.

SONIA

You? What are you . . . doing so far from home?

OLD WOMAN

I might ask you the same question.

Sonia suspiciously regards the Old Woman, who moves past her, holding her gnarled hand out to a young Black Woman who has settled on to the bench, unwrapping a sandwich for her dinner.

Spare a little change for an old woman who's been too long on her tired feet.

YOUNG WOMAN
(*shaking her head*)

Sorry.

The Old Woman nods. Then she leans over, and touches *the young woman's ear.*

OLD WOMAN

Nice earrings.

The Young Woman forces a smile. As the Old Woman straightens up and begins to shuffle away, the camera closes in on the Young Woman's ear.

Sonia's eyes slowly widen. Her face fills with nervous excitement. She sidles up closer to the Young Woman.

SONIA

Excuse me . . . those earrings *are* beautiful.

YOUNG WOMAN

Thanks.

SONIA

Would you mind if I took a closer look?

The Young Woman shrugs her shoulders, resigned to an afternoon of weirdness. Sonia pulls out her loupe *and puts it right to the Young Woman's ear, who sits there, wondering what the hell is going on.*

Might I ask you how you came by these?

YOUNG WOMAN

Listen, lady – I'm glad you like them, but they're not valuable or nothing. There's this guy who makes them, in my neighborhood. It's just a neighborhood guy who makes nice stuff.

SONIA

What neighborhood?

CUT TO:

EXT. BUSHWICK, BROOKLYN. ELEVATED TRAIN STATION — DUSK

The 'El' train pulls out of the station, and we boom down until we are on:

Sonia, who walks down the stairs to the sidewalk and steps out on to the bustling avenue of Broadway. The sounds of salsa and Latin rhythms play from within the stores all around her, as she heads up the teeming avenue.

INT. GARCIA HOME — DUSK

A door swings open, revealing Sonia's anxious face. She smiles tentatively.

> SONIA
>
> Hello?

REVERSE ON: the face Jasmina Garcia, a short Hispanic woman in her late middle-age. She speaks only in Spanish:

> MRS GARCIA
>
> *Buenos dias.*

> SONIA
>
> I'm looking for a jeweller – I was given this address.

Mrs Garcia doesn't understand. Sonia points at her own finger, miming putting on a ring . . .

> Jeweller . . . jewelry maker.

> MRS GARCIA
>
> *Ah, si, si. Entra, por favor.*

She motions Sonia inside, closing the door behind her. The room is extremely dark, lit by the flames from dozens of candles.

Sonia's POV. The walls and shelves are completely covered with Catholic paraphernalia – ornate crucifixes, paintings of Jesus and Mary, rosaries and every other kind of goyish chachke.

Mrs Garcia opens a side door and motions for Sonia to enter. Sonia nods and steps through the doorway.

INT. STAIRWELL – DUSK

Dollying shot – from Sonia's POV – descending the dark stairwell, then coming out into:

INT. RAMON'S STUDIO – DUSK

An intensely cluttered space filled with an incredible array of sculptures – shafts of light streaming through multicolored stained-glass windows illuminate unfinished-looking works ranging from the romantic to the most modern of styles. It is also a workshop and several wooden tables are covered with masses of ironworking tools and implements. And, most incredibly of all:

Ramon is crouched over a table in the middle of the room. There is a blow-pipe in his lips, from which he is directing a hot blue flame on to a tiny piece of metal which he is soldering. He puts down the pipe, dips the piece of metal into a cup of water and raises it to:

The ear of a teenage Latino Homegirl, whose two Friends are standing in the open doorway to the yard beyond the studio.

> HOMEGIRL
> Yo, I wanted one like Charlene's.

> RAMON
> This is better, it suits your face.

Sonia steps slowly into the strange, colorful space, staring at Ramon in disbelief.

> HOMEGIRL
> How much you want for it?

> RAMON
> The reward of seeing it on such a lovely ear is all I could ask for.

> VOICE
> (off-screen)
> Yo, Ramon!

Sonia's POV sweeps over to the corner, where a Young Man and Woman, both of them stark naked, are reclining on a mattress in front of an unfinished sculpture of their intertwined forms.

YOUNG WOMAN
I been sitting my naked ass over here three weekends in a
row, you ain't paid me jack and you turning down her dollars?

The Homegirl grins as she walks back to her Friends.

HOMEGIRL
That's 'cause your fat ass ain't worth my dollars, homegirl.

YOUNG WOMAN
Yo, the hell with this, alright?

She gets up and grabs a robe, then stalks across the room right past:

Sonia, on whose stunned face we hold, as:

*Ramon stares at her with narrowed eyes. He's at least twice as surprised
to see her as she is him. They exchange a very strange look.*

*Then Ramon reaches into his pocket, finds some cash and walks over to
where Ty, the naked young man, is pulling on his trousers.*

RAMON
Here, Ty . . . take this for now. Talk to her, alright? I need
you guys.

TY
Yo, it's cold in here, man.

RAMON
I know, just one more time, alright?

*Ty nods and he and Ramon give each other skin. There is an off-screen
sound and Ramon turns:*

*Sonia has bumped into one of the sculptures, which she steadies with her
hands.*

Ramon takes a step forward, expression tense.

Let me guess. You didn't quite succeed in getting my ass
fired at work today, so you followed me home to make sure
my life is a living hell here as well.

                                SONIA

    Not exactly.

An awkward silence.

    You're . . . quite a collector.

Ramon gestures at the sculptures:

                                RAMON

    You mean these?

Sonia nods.

    Not exactly. I mean, not on purpose. I make them. Nobody
    buys any, so I guess I'm collecting them.

*Sonia looks at an array of unfinished jewelry spread out on the table in
front of her.*

                                SONIA

    What about these?

                                RAMON

    Stuff I sell to the neighborhood girls for some pocket money.
    Mostly metal shavings from my sculptures. Worthless.

                                SONIA

    Worthless?

She looks right at Ramon.

    This is art.

Ramon looks at Sonia curiously, with a sudden intensity, then:

                                 TY

    Yo, Ray, peace.

Ramon turns toward the young man, who is leaving the studio.

                                RAMON

    Peace, Ty. Later, alright?

*Sonia looks around the room, her eyes traveling over the unfinished
sculptures all around her.*

SONIA

You have an . . . interesting style, Ramon.

RAMON

It's not really no style. They're just mostly unfinished. I get
an idea, you know, get all hot over it, then when I'm halfway
through, I can't remember why I started. But thanks.

Sonia is silent. Ramon looks her over for a moment, then:

What brings you to my neck of the woods, Miss . . . *Mrs*
Horowitz?

Sonia reaches into her purse and takes out the gold ring.

Ramon's eyes widen.

SONIA

It was in a pile of junk Kapoor was going to sell to the
melters. It's yours, isn't it?

RAMON
(*nodding*)

I don't know how . . . It must'a got mixed up in there,
somehow . . . Jesus.

SONIA

This is 24 carat gold.

RAMON

When I come across some cheap alloy, I melt it down and
separate out the gold. That's as pure an alloy as you're gonna
get without it turning into a beautiful piece of chewing gum.

Sonia holds the ring out to Ramon.

SONIA

Whatever stone you had in it is gone. I'm sorry.

RAMON

It was never there.

He takes the ring from her hand.

I made this for my muse.

SONIA

Who?

RAMON

My muse. My inspiration.

SONIA

And . . . who is she?

RAMON

I don't know. But when I meet her, I will know. And I'll know exactly what stone to put in the heart of my ring.

SONIA

It looks to me like you already have all the inspiration that you need.

Ramon smiles slightly. He closes his hand around the ring.

RAMON

Thank you.

SONIA

Ramon . . .

She pauses, as he looks at her questioningly.

Kapoor doesn't have a clue, does he? Does anyone in the trade know?

RAMON

Know what?

SONIA

What you do.

Ramon suddenly looks nervous. He turns and walks back to his sculpture in progress and begins gathering his materials.

RAMON

Listen – I got a *job*. All this stuff – it's just a hobby. It's a distraction. That's all.

SONIA

You see the garbage that passes through that store everyday – have you really looked at any other designers' work recently? Just to compare styles – check out the competition?

RAMON

I'm not in a competition.

Sonia studies Ramon for a moment and finally decides.

SONIA

I want to commission your designs.

Ramon stops what he is doing. He keeps his eyes on the floor.

Ramon, I'm not certified, but I'm as fine a gemmologist as you'll ever meet.

RAMON

Or ever hope to.

SONIA

And I don't know from sculpture – but other than a few Florentine antiques that passed through my father's hands for appraisal, I've never seen any jewelry as – beautiful – as yours in all my life. I have been buying and selling the same dull old garbage to an extremely wealthy clientele that would drink up your work like a thirsty man in a desert. I have access to the finest materials and stones. Please consider my offer.

Ramon straightens up and slowly walks over to Sonia.

RAMON

I'm very . . . moved . . . by your passion, Mrs . . .

SONIA

Sonia.

RAMON

I am moved, Sonia. But we hardly know each other. And I can't help wondering if you want to do this for me – or if you want this for you.

They are very close to one another. Sonia hesitates for a moment. Then:

SONIA

Does it matter?

Ramon looks closely at her, thinking it over.

CUT TO:

INT. HOROWITZ APARTMENT – NIGHT

The front door creaks open and Sonia steps into the foyer. She takes off her coat and hangs it up, then stops in front of the hallway mirror. She is now wearing a pair of Ramon's earrings. She turns her head slightly, admiring them . . . then touches her neck, where hanging over her buttoned-up collar is a lovely necklace. As she touches it, she also models the bracelet newly adorning her wrist. Then:

VOICE
(*off-screen*)

Sonia.

She nearly hops out of her skin in surprise. She steps into the living-room and switches on the light.

Mendel is sitting on the sofa, hands clasped . . . waiting.

SONIA

Mendel? What are you doing out here lurking in the dark?
(*no answer*)
Where's Shimmie?

MENDEL

By Rachel.

Sonia looks at her watch.

SONIA

Oy gevalt . . . I better go get him . . .

She turns back to the foyer, but:

MENDEL

He'll be all right.

Sonia ignores him, reaching for her coat . . .
(*shouting*)
I said he'll be . . .

Sonia freezes. Mendel finishes the sentence softly:

. . . all right.

Silence. Sonia turns and faces Mendel.

Where have you been?

SONIA

Working.

Mendel gets up off the sofa and walks over to where Sonia is standing. He touches her ear, her throat.

MENDEL

What's all this?

SONIA

They're . . . samples, from a jeweler I'm going to be representing. It's part of my work for Sender.

Mendel nods, then:

MENDEL

I told Sender you won't be working for him anymore.

Sonia is stunned.

MENDEL

I've asked him to replace you as soon as possible.

SONIA

What did Sender say?

MENDEL

What did *Sender* say? I'm your husband, Sonia – by you Sender does what I ask. I told him you're needed here at home, and that was the end of it.

Sonia is on the verge of exploding, but all she manages is:

SONIA

All the women around here work.

MENDEL

They work, but their husbands don't get snickered at by everyone in the neighborhood as soon as his back is turned.

SONIA

Why should they be snickering?

MENDEL

If I knew, I wouldn't be sitting here asking you about it.

SONIA

Is that what you're doing? Asking me about it?

Mendel grimaces, in agony.

MENDEL

Sonia, I know you've got – *we've* got – problems. I talked about it with some people who know about these things, and . . .

Sonia starts to protest, but Mendel overrides her.

Please, Sonia. I realize I've been too busy at the Yeshiva, and with my own learning, to give you the kind of attention you deserve. I also understand that we're both in desperate need of help right now.

SONIA
(*suspicious*)

What kind of help?

MENDEL

I'd like for us to see a counsellor.

SONIA

A what?

MENDEL

A marriage counsellor. A psychologist who specializes in problems married people are having. It's an impartial expert who'll help you – us – to understand things more clearly.

Sonia looks closely at her husband, carefully considering it.

CUT TO:

INT. PSYCHOLOGIST'S OFFICE – DAY

Dr Bauer, a bearded Hassidic man wearing a large black yarmulke, who looks exactly like a younger version of the Rebbe, presses his fingers together and asks:

DR BAUER
Do you pray every morning, Mrs Horowitz?

Sonia and Mendel are sitting side by side across the desk from the doctor. Sonia looks confused.

SONIA
Excuse me?

DR BAUER
Do you pray every morning?

SONIA
I thought you were . . .
> (*to Mendel*)

You said he was . . .
> (*to the doctor*)

I thought you were a psychologist.

DR BAUER
Board certified.

SONIA
Then what's all this about praying?

DR BAUER
I am a psychologist, Mrs Horowitz, and I am also a rabbi, uniquely qualified to appreciate the problems afflicting the Jewish soul, which is unique in that it is directly connected to the spirit of the Holy One, blessed be his Name.

Sonia starts to say something, but Mendel puts his hand on hers:

MENDEL
Sonia, give the doctor a chance.

Sonia simmers down. She removes her hand from under Mendel's and squeezes her hands together, waiting.

DR BAUER
Have you been praying, Mrs Horowitz?

SONIA
No.

DR BAUER

Have you been to the *mikveh?*

SONIA

Not this month.

DR BAUER

Are you lighting shabbes candles?

SONIA

If I get in on time.

DR BAUER

Have you been keeping kosher?

SONIA

At home.

MENDEL

At *home?*

DR BAUER
(bangs his desk)

Now we're getting somewhere.

SONIA

Where exactly are we getting?

DR BAUER

It's clear that you've been neglecting your relationship with the Almighty, which in psychological terms has translated into . . .

SONIA

(*to Mendel*)

I thought you said he was going to be impartial.

MENDEL

Whose side is he taking? I don't see . . .

SONIA

He's taking God's side, that's whose side he's taking.

DR BAUER

One can't choose sides with the Lord, Mrs Horowitz, one can only . . .

SONIA

You – don't tell me what I can or can't do. I'll pick any side I want, and if God happens to be on the other end, then that's just the way it's gonna be.

Mendel reaches for Sonia's hand again, his eyes full of pained confusion.

MENDEL

Sonia, the way you talk sometimes . . . don't you fear the Lord?

SONIA

Sure I fear him. I also fear the drug dealers on the corner of 33rd Avenue, but am I gonna run around all day doing everything they tell me to? No. I am going to cross to the other side of the street and hope they leave me alone, that's what I'm gonna do.

DR BAUER

And if they don't leave you alone, Mrs Horowitz?

SONIA

Then I'll get down on my knees and beg for my life.
(*stands up*)
And if I'm still alive when it's over, I'll go home, pack my
bags and move to a nicer neighborhood.

DR BAUER

There is no escaping God, Mrs Horowitz.

SONIA

Then let him do what he wants to me. I really don't care
anymore.

MENDEL

And our child, Sonia? Your son. Don't you care about him?

SONIA

So now he's gonna take it out on Shimmie? What is he, this
God of yours, an extortionist? I didn't realize when I lit
shabbes candles on Friday night I was paying protection to
some kind of heavenly Al Capone.

MENDEL

(*shaking his head*)
How can you be so blind? Don't you see what kind of
suffering you're asking for?

SONIA

Mendel, my learned husband – we don't suffer because we
ask for it. We suffer because that's just the way it is. There's
no reason for it. And if there is, it's certainly something
neither you or this board certified idiot have a clue about.

MENDEL

We bring suffering on *ourselves*, Sonia. Because we sin against
God.

SONIA

Really? And my uncles and aunts and all their children who
were marched into the gas chambers in Treblinka? My aunt
Chani who watched her son tortured right in front of her
eyes? What the hell did they do to deserve that? And Yossi
. . . What did he do that was so . . . What did he do . . .?

There are tears in Sonia's eyes, as she chokes on her sorrow, unable to continue.

MENDEL
(*confused*)

Yossi?

DR BAUER

We don't question the ways of God, Mrs Horowitz. We just . . .

SONIA

No, *you* don't question them, Dr Rabbi – or is it Rabbi Doctor? Who cares? I'm gonna question whatever I want to. But since I'm not likely to get any answers in this lifetime . . .

She turns, grabs her coat and stalks out of the room, slamming the door shut.

CUT TO:

We see Mendel's tormented face in the doorway of his brother's house.

MENDEL

Is Sender home?

Feiga, Sender's wife, looks at her brother-in-law with concern.

FEIGA

Mendel, are you all right?

Mendel steps into the foyer.

MENDEL

Is my brother home?

FEIGA

Sure . . . yes, he's in his study. Come wait in the living-room – I'll go get him.

She leads Mendel into the living-room, where a slew of Sender's Children are spread out, reading and playing board games. They immediately greet Mendel in cacophonous good cheer.

Hey, uncle Mendel! Come on and play! Know what I learned in
school today? Uncle Mendel . . .

Feiga steps in and barks:

FEIGA

Shah! Everyone to their rooms! On the double – double-time
march! *Let's go let's go let's go!*

*She claps vigorously, and the kids hop up and hurry out of the living-
room. Mendel sits down on the sofa, hands clasped tightly together,
rocking back and forth. A dark-clad figure steps into the frame in the
foreground and Mendel looks up. His face is drawn in agony.*

MENDEL

Why?

CLOSE ON: *Sender standing in the entrance to the living-room. His eyes
narrow in response to the question.*

SENDER

Why what?

MENDEL

Why is this happening?

*Sender relaxes a little. He walks into the room and stands over his
miserable brother.*

SENDER

What's happening, Mendel?

MENDEL

Sonia's gone crazy.

SENDER

Crazy?

MENDEL

She's running around like a *meschuggener* – saying such things
I don't even know where she gets them from, about God,
about who knows what . . . I don't even know what she's
talking about anymore.

SENDER

She's just sounds a little wound up. I'm sure she'll calm down soon.

Tears glitter in Mendel's eyes. He shakes his head.

MENDEL

What have I done? What have I done wrong?

He looks up at his brother.

What have I done?

SENDER

Nothing.

He puts a hand on Mendel's shoulder.

You're a *tzaddik*, Mendel.

MENDEL

Then why is this happening to me?

SENDER

Because you've never done anything wrong.

Mendel shakes his head; he can't understand. But he grasps Sender's hands tightly, and looks up at him imploringly . . .

MENDEL

I don't know what to do, Sender. Please . . . help me.

CUT TO:

INT. BASEMENT 'STORE' – DAY

A suitcase is opened, revealing a display of Ramon's jewelry laid out against a black velvet backing.

SONIA
(*off-screen*)

This is an excellent representative selection of the designer's skill and versatility, Mr Berman.

Mr Berman, a well-tailored man with a refined air about him, is sitting

86

across the desk from Sonia and a fidgeting, extremely uncomfortable-looking Ramon. Berman picks up a brooch and examines it with his loupe.

Due to financial constraints, Mr Garcia has been working primarily with inexpensive materials, as you can see. But I think you'll find the delicacy and balance of his work as stunning as I do.

Mr Berman picks up a bracelet and turns it in his fingers.

MR BERMAN
Yes – but I'm not quite sure exactly what style I'm looking at. It's somewhat classical, Florentine almost, but then it's also . . .

He looks to Ramon for some explanation. Ramon smiles apologetically, trying to find words, but he is frozen by his nervousness; then Sonia leans in:

SONIA
. . . a touch modern. I know, Mr Berman, it's a little confusing. To someone with just a smidgen of taste, but not enough of it, this work might border on kitsch. But there's a

purity in the Florentine influence and a boldness to the
modern flourishes that totally belies that.

*Sonia brushes back a strand of hair that is falling out from under the
kerchief covering her head and shows Mr Berman the earrings she is
wearing.*

It also enhances . . . the appearance of the wearer without
drawing undue attention to itself . . .
    (*showing the necklace hanging outside her collar*)
I apologize for lack of a better model but with some
imagination, I think you'll see a world of possibilities.

MR BERMAN

Yes . . . and without as much imagination as you might think.

*Sonia blushes slightly; then she reaches into her pocket and takes out the
gold ring.*

SONIA

Here's an example of his work in fine metals. 24 carat gold.
It's hand-carved – one of a kind – with an open setting for a
gemstone. The perfection of this piece is clear even to the
naked eye.

*Mr Berman takes the ring. Sonia and Ramon exchange a look as Mr
Berman carefully inspects it.*

MR BERMAN

I'm inclined to agree with you, Mrs Horowitz. If you can bear
to part with these samples, I'd like to show them to my
partners. I'd also like yourself and Mr . . .?

*Berman trails off. It's a moment before Ramon realizes he's being talked
about.*

RAMON

Garcia . . . Ramon Garcia.

MR BERMAN

Yes. I'd like you to meet my manufacturer. He's in town
every Thursday. We can make an appointment in a couple of
weeks if you have the . . .

SONIA

This week.

Mr Berman is a little taken aback. Sonia tries to hide her desperation under a smile.

This week would be best.

MR BERMAN

I'll see what I can do.

Sonia nods gratefully and starts to close the suitcase . . . then she stops and takes out the gold ring.

SONIA

I'll just . . . hold on to this piece, Mr Berman. If you don't mind. It's one of a kind, and . . . well, I'm sure they'll be able to see what they need to see from the rest of the selection.

Mr Berman looks at Sonia from under a raised eyebrow.

CUT TO:

The wall safe is being opened. Sonia's hands place the gold ring inside, then shut the safe again.

CUT TO:

INT. RAMON'S WORKSHOP – DAY

A small avalanche of gold jewelry spills out on to a worktable . . . Tilt up to reveal Sonia, as she speaks hurriedly, her voice tinged with barely suppressed anxiety.

SONIA

– The meeting went just . . . well, great. It couldn't have gone better . . .

Ramon is kneeling over his sculpture of a man intertwined with a woman, angrily molding the plaster with his hands. Ty, the nude male model, is posing alone on the mattress in front of him, but the young woman is conspicuously absent.

RAMON

I looked like an idiot.

SONIA

Don't be crazy, you were just a little nervous. It was
charming. Any talking needs to be done, that's what I'm there
for . . .

*Sonia avoids looking at the naked Ty as she walks over to Ramon. She
passes Ramon's mother, who is dusting one of the sculptures with a rag
– Mrs Garcia dips her hand into a cup and sprinkles the sculpture with
water from her fingers; after which she closes her eyes and crosses herself.*

(*to Ramon*)

Trust me. He was trying to play it cool, but his eyes were
popping out of his head. We'll have an appointment with the
manufacturer this week or . . .

RAMON

(*interrupting*)

Damn, can you believe this?

Sonia is confused. He indicates Ty, alone on the mattress.

She bugged out on me, and I couldn't find anyone to replace
her. I'm getting it, though . . .

SONIA

It's, uh, very nice.

RAMON

Nice, huh. You hear that, Ty? You look nice.

*Sonia can't help sneaking a sideways glance at Ty, who catches her
look, and smiles.*

Sonia's eyes instantly look away. Her face is red.

SONIA

The sculpture looks nice.

*She is standing right beside Ramon's mother; who sprinkles another
sculpture with water and crosses herself.*

Sonia looks to Ramon, who shrugs:

RAMON

Don't ask.

He gestures at the jewelry on the tabletop:

What's all this?

SONIA

Gold *chachkes*. Junk.

RAMON

I can see that. What I mean is; why is it all over my table?

SONIA

You can melt it all down and start working on a set of unique
pieces to augment your portfolio. I'm going to sell them for
prices you can't even begin to imagine . . .

RAMON

Sonia, I hardly have enough time to . . .

SONIA

I know – that's why I brought you these resumés.

She holds out a sheaf of papers.

RAMON

Resumés?

SONIA

Potential assistants. They've all been highly recommended,
but I know when you meet with them in person you'll form
your own opinion about their . . .

RAMON

Whoa – whoa – *whoa* –

Sonia stops.

RAMON
(*insecure*)
I got a job to hold on to. A real fuckin' job. I *told* you this is
just a hobby.

SONIA

You seem to be working on it pretty hard, for just a hobby.

*Ramon is silent. Then the tension is momentarily broken by Mrs
Garcia, who asks Ramon a question in Spanish.*

RAMON

No thanks, Mami . . .
(*to Sonia*)
You want a cup of coffee?

*Sonia shakes her head. Mrs Garcia turns and walks toward the
stairwell leading upstairs.*

Ramon turns back to his sculpture.

SONIA

We agreed that I would represent your work, and in order for
me to do that I need a base to start building on.

RAMON

I gave you those samples to show and that was it. But
meetings, portfolios, assistants . . . I'll never be able to keep
up with my work for Kapoor like that.

SONIA

Quit.

Ramon looks up sharply at Sonia.

SONIA

You've got your real work cut out for you – just haven't
accepted it yet.

RAMON

Hey, who *are* you, lady? I mean, I just met you, and you come
busting in here like your ass is on fire, telling me how to live
my life?

SONIA

You want to go on like this? Wasting your talent, working for
some cheap junk *macher* day in and day out, just so you can
hold on to some lousy 'job'?

RAMON

I don't know where *you* come from, but around here that's a
fuckin' hell of a lot more than most people got. So don't go
laughing it off like it ain't shit.

TY

(*off-screen*)

Yo, this is getting too deep for my shivering ass. I'm a leave
you two to . . .

RAMON

Stay right there, alright? We ain't done yet.

Sonia looks at Ramon with desperate eyes . . .

SONIA

You're an artist, Ramon. I just want . . . to help you.

Ramon works over his plaster cast, grimacing in frustration . . .

RAMON

Yo, Ty, that's not how you were. Why you keep shifting
around, man?

TY

I can't hold it without her here, homes.

Ramon stops. He turns to Sonia.

RAMON

You want to help me? Come over here for a minute.

Sonia looks confused. Ramon steps over and starts leading her to the mattress where Ty is posing.

SONIA

Where . . .? What do you think . . . no. No, absolutely not.

RAMON

Just a minute, so I can get this angle right.

Sonia's eyes are desperately avoiding looking at Ty's body, as they stop near the mattress.

SONIA

I really shouldn't be so close to . . .

RAMON

Hey, it isn't really you – it's art, remember? Just use your imagination. This is the Garden of Eden. There's no shame here. This is Adam . . .

SONIA

Shouldn't he be wearing a fig leaf or something?

Ramon guides Sonia down to the mattress beside Ty, and starts to position her.

RAMON

. . . and you're Eve.

SONIA

I suppose that makes you the snake.

RAMON

The devil in disguise.

SONIA

Well, Mr Snake, I hate to break it to you, but this Eve is keeping her clothes on.

Sonia's hand grasps Ramon's. Squeezes it in supplication. He could stop right there . . . but he doesn't, lowering Sonia's hand to the mattress.

RAMON

That's alright . . . Move your arm just like that . . .

Sonia is becoming more enmeshed with Ty, her face growing damp with nervous sweat . . . then she can't take it anymore. She yanks away from Ramon and scrambles to her feet.

She looks back at Ramon, then turns, grabs her bag and storms out of the studio . . .

HOLD ON: *Ramon watching her go with a pained expression.*

TY
(off-screen)

Smooth, homes.

EXT. STREET. BUSHWICK – DAY

Sonia is hurrying up the crowded sidewalk, heading for the 'El', when:

RAMON
(off-screen)

Sonia!

She keeps walking. Ramon is running up the street behind her. He catches up, panting.

I'm sorry, Sonia . . . I can't believe I did that to you . . .

Sonia keeps walking.

It's just that you fuckin' scare me, alright?

Sonia turns and faces Ramon.

SONIA

My father used to say a jeweler's work was the expression of his soul. Your work is beautiful, Ramon – but what's the point if nobody's gonna know it?

RAMON

You'll know.

There is a silent moment between them. Then:

Sounds like you had a wise old man. I never knew mine. My mother ain't got nobody in the world but me and Jesus Christ – and He don't seem to be making no grocery runs these

95

days, know what I'm saying? How do I know you're gonna come through for me?

SONIA

You don't. But that's life, isn't it?

Ramon takes that in; and finally nods.

RAMON

Just give me a little time.

SONIA

I'm running out of time.

She forces a bitter smile, then turns and walks away.

CLOSE ON: *Ramon watching Sonia go, standing alone in the middle of the sidewalk.*

Panning with Sonia as she crosses the street and heads toward the subway . . . The moving camera stops on:

A black sedan parked at the curb. The figure in the driver's seat is looking out of the car window. Rack focus to reveal:

Sender, who lights a cigarette, and takes a few thoughtful puffs. He reaches for the ignition, starts the car and pulls away.

CUT TO:

INT. APARTMENT BUILDING. HALLWAY – EVENING

Sonia comes out of the stairwell, walks down the corridor, and stops in front of the door to her apartment. She hesitates for a moment, then finds her keys and tries to put them into the lock. They don't work. She tries another key. No dice. She tries to force it, but nothing happens.

Sonia rings the bell. No answer. She bangs on the door with her fist.

SONIA

Mendel?

Still no response. She rings again, jabbing at the buzzer in frustration.

CUT TO:

INT. FEINBERG HOME – EVENING

Sonia is in the hallway, facing Rachel and her anxious-looking husband Schmuel.

> SONIA
>
> The locks to my house have been changed.

> RACHEL
>
> You've hardly set a foot in that door for months and suddenly it's your house?

> SONIA
>
> Where's Shimmie?

> RACHEL
>
> Sleeping.

Sonia takes a step forward, but Rachel blocks her way.

> SONIA
>
> Don't get between me and my baby.

> RACHEL
>
> Your baby? You've hardly seen hide or hair of him for months, now suddenly he's your baby?

> SONIA
>
> You sound like a broken record, Rachel.

> RACHEL
>
> Sit down.

Schmuel clears his throat.

> SCHMUEL
>
> Uh, ladies, I think it might be a good idea if you. . .

> RACHEL
>
> Put on your coat, round up the kids and take them to *daven mairiv* at schul, Schmuel.

> SCHMUEL
>
> Right. That's what I was going to do. Schul.

He quickly heads off to gather his kids. Rachel turns back to Sonia:

RACHEL

You better sit down.

Sonia hesitates, then grudgingly sits down in a chair across from Rachel.

RACHEL

It's over. Mendel will be granting you a divorce at the earliest possible moment.

Sonia is stunned. Her mouth tries to form words, but nothing comes out.

He's going to stay in the house. Sender has agreed to let you use an apartment he's been keeping for business on the Lower East Side. You're not welcome here anymore.

SONIA

Is this coming from Mendel – or is this coming from you?

RACHEL

What do you think?

SONIA

Where is Mendel? I want to hear this from his mouth.

RACHEL

Don't you think you've already put him through enough?

Sonia takes that in; then makes her decision. She stands back up:

SONIA

I'll take Shimmie and be on my way.

RACHEL

Shimmie stays here.

SONIA

How . . . dare you?

RACHEL

Shimmie's going to stay here by us, where he can live in a healthy environment.

SONIA

And who's the expert fit to judge what's a healthy environment all of a sudden?

98

RACHEL

Certainly not a woman who leaves her husband and child at home so she can run around town having affairs with Puerto Ricans.

Sonia is dumbfounded.

SONIA

Where did you . . .? Is that what this is all about?
(*no answer*)
Who said this?

RACHEL

It doesn't matter. What's done is done.

SONIA

And what's said is said, and the truth doesn't matter anymore, does it?

Rachel is silent.

If you don't get out of my way, I'm gonna call the cops. I'm taking Shimmie and I'm going to go back to Monsey to stay by my mother.

RACHEL

We already spoke to your mother.

Sonia's brain is reeling . . . Rachel is too far ahead of her.

She begged us not to let you go back there and ruin your sisters' chances of making decent matches. This is going to be hard enough on your family's reputation without you making a star appearance and flaunting yourself for everyone to see.

SONIA

What is this – some kind of conspiracy?

RACHEL

We have a fine life here, Sonia. A decent life. And you're not going to be allowed to destroy it for everyone around you. For the good of all concerned – you've got to be cut off.

SONIA

You can't cut a mother off from her child.

99

                              RACHEL
No. You've already taken care of that yourself.

Tears well in Sonia's eyes, as she takes in the accusation.

A child needs more than just a mother in order to flourish. It
needs a stable home, a decent family. A caring community.
You know that as well as I do.

Sonia is silent under Rachel's severe glare.

I don't know where you're headed, Sonia, but wherever it is
. . . you're going alone.

CUT TO:

INT. SYNAGOGUE. LOBBY — EVENING

*Sonia stalks through the crowded lobby until she is at the entrance to the
besmedresh – past which no women are allowed. She scans the sea of
black-clad men, then turns to a Young Hassid standing by the doorway.*

                              SONIA
Is Mendel here? Mendel Horowitz?

The Young Hassid shrugs, annoyed.

Do me a favor and find him for me, will you? Tell him his
wife wants to see him.

*The Young Hassid turns and heads into the crush of bodies packing the
besmedresh.*

*Sonia waits impatiently by the doorway. She looks around, and notices
that everyone in the lobby is eyeing her strangely.*

*A clique of women casts furtive glances in her direction and whisper to
one another as they head up the stairs to the women's balcony.*

                              VOICE
                          (off-screen)
Excuse me . . .

The Young Hassid has reappeared in the doorway.

I think you should find another time for this.

Is he here?

Like I said, another time would be prefer–

Sonia brushes past him, walking right into the besmedresh. *We dolly with her as she passes through the throng of men, all whom 'tcth!' and mumble loudly in a chorus of disapproval.*

Sonia keeps walking until she has reached Mendel, stopping behind him. He stands in the foreground, eyes closed, praying fervently.

Mendel.

Mendel ignores her, squeezing his eyes shut tighter, focusing on his prayer with increased fervor.

Is this it, Mendel? Is this how you want to handle things?

No response. A few young men move in between Sonia and Mendel – careful not to touch her, but motioning angrily at her to move.

Sonia glares at Mendel for a moment, then turns, shoves aside one of the young men and strides out of the besmedresh.

HOLD ON: *Mendel's face, eyes tightly shut, lips moving rapidly, trying to drown out the world with the intensity of his prayers.*

CUT TO:

EXT. FRONT STOOP. 'STORE' – NIGHT

Sonia hurries up the street and turns on to the walkway leading to the front door, but is stopped by Nelson.

> NELSON
> Sorry, Mrs Horowitz, store's off limits.

> SONIA
> What are you talking about?

> NELSON
> Mr Sender's orders. I can't let you inside.

> SONIA
> Listen to me, Nelson. There are things that belong to me in there. They are mine. I will go in, get them and be out in ten minutes.

> NELSON
> Can't do it. Good night, Mrs Horowitz.

CUT TO:

An elevated tram across the screen, descending into a dark subway tunnel as it crosses from Brooklyn into Manhattan.

INT. SUBWAY CAR – NIGHT

Sonia sits squeezed in between the passengers in the crowded car. Her eyes are burning with emotion and for a moment it looks like she is about to break down . . . but she sets her face in grim determination and holds it back. Not yet.

CUT TO:

INT. LOWER EAST SIDE TENEMENT. LOBBY – NIGHT

The front door opens a crack and Sonia's face becomes partially visible. She tries to open the door all the way, but it won't budge. She pushes with all her might, forcing it in . . . and looks down. Pan down to reveal:

A sleeping Drunk on the floor, wedged in between the door and the wall. Sonia's feet step over him and she walks into the tiny lobby and checks out the list of apartment numbers. She wrinkles her nose in distaste and heads up the graffiti-covered stairwell.

INT. TENEMENT APARTMENT – NIGHT

Sonia steps into the small, dingy living-room, and looks around . . . A chair, a bed, that's all. As she walks around the cramped space, we see that there is a figure behind her, framed in the kitchen doorway.

                    FIGURE
Welcome home.

Sonia almost jumps out of her skin. She turns around:

Sender is standing there. He smiles.

                    SONIA
'An apartment he keeps for business' your sister says. I
wonder how she'd feel if she knew what kind of transactions
occurred here.

Sender walks over to the chair and sits down. He gestures to the bed.

                    SENDER
Make yourself comfortable.

                    SONIA
A bed, Sender? I would have expected a desk, or a table – or
maybe just the wall. Who'd have thought you'd have time for
a bed?

                    SENDER
Your bitter tone strikes me as inappropriate, considering that
I've given you exactly what you want.

SONIA

And what exactly is that? A rathole in a crackhouse on the
Lower East Side?

SENDER

Your freedom.

Sender gets up and walks over to Sonia. He puts his face close to hers.

You're free of Mendel. You're free of all the everyday
responsibilities that you hate. You're free to work at a trade
you enjoy and live in any manner you wish. Free.

SONIA

And you, Sender? Am I free of you?

SENDER

Freedom always comes with a price.

SONIA

And what is your price?

SENDER

A price above that of your virtue – but a price far below
rubies.

He leans in and touches his lips to her cheek, then kisses her full on the mouth. She returns his embrace for a moment . . . then she gently pushes him back. She looks closely at Sender and slowly shakes her head.

You'll have nothing, Sonia. Not even this room. Nothing.

Sonia's face tightens. A slight, bitter smile of understanding plays in her eyes, and she moves away from Sender. She walks to the door, opens it and stops there.

SONIA

I'm not paying anymore.

She turns and leaves the apartment.

HOLD ON: *Sender's face, his dark eyes glittering in the dim light as the door clicks shut.*

CUT TO:

EXT. LOWER EAST SIDE. PAYPHONE – NIGHT

Long lens on Sonia standing at the public phone on a street corner, traffic whizzing by all around her. We can catch only fragments of the conversation she is having over the sound of speeding motors.

SONIA

Yes . . . she told me, Mother . . . Rachel told me that she talked to you, but I wanted to make sure for myself that . . . No, Mother, don't worry . . . I won't be coming home . . . don't worry . . .

CUT TO:

EXT. LOWER EAST SIDE STREETS – NIGHT

Sonia walks down the street on the verge of tears. The camera dollies in front of her . . . until someone bumps into her so hard it spins her around.

VOICE

What's the rush?

A silhouette emerges into the light. It's the Old Beggar Woman.

OLD WOMAN

Late for a party?

SONIA

I'm lost.

OLD WOMAN

You're in the middle of Manhattan, on the corner of 3rd Street and 2nd Avenue. The J train is three blocks east of here and the IRT is just around the corner. Nobody is lost here.

Sonia carefully regards the Old Woman.

SONIA

Who are you?

OLD WOMAN

Just an old woman who's been moving for too long on her tired old feet. But I'm going to rest, now. Will you join me?

Sonia hesitates.

You got any better offers?

Sonia shakes her head.

Don't worry – I don't bite. And even if I did . . .

Her mouth cracks into a black, toothless grin.

CUT TO:

INT. ROOM. ABANDONED BUILDING – NIGHT

Sonia sits across from the Old Woman, who strikes a match and drops it into a tin can filled with loose sticks.

SONIA

You've been following me – since the day I arrived in Boro Park.

The tin can, which begins to glow with orange flames, warmly illuminates the women's faces.

OLD WOMAN

It's you who has been following me.

Sonia's eyes are wide with anxiety. The Old Woman touches Sonia's cheek and Sonia flinches.

What are you so afraid of, *meidaleh?*

SONIA

The devil.

OLD WOMAN

Oh, yes. And where is this devil?

SONIA

Here . . . in me. It's been burning me away slowly from the inside out. I have nothing left.

OLD WOMAN

You have your fear.
(*grins*)
I know a thing or two about the devil, myself . . .

The fire dances in the old woman's eyes.

She is old. As old as God himself. She's very beautiful and she is very wise. But we fear and hate her, when we should be making her our trusted ally.

(*leaning toward Sonia*)

It makes her bitter and vengeful – so she burns us with the flames of her spite. She's sensitive and not very forgiving . . . but if you learn to embrace her, you will have made a valuable friend.

SONIA

And God?

OLD WOMAN

(*sighs*)

Better to stay on his good side too.

SONIA

I think it's a little late for that, in my case.

OLD WOMAN

Ahh. He's an old bully, and it's best to keep bullies in their places, I say.

SONIA

Even the big ones?

The Old Woman begins to chuckle.

OLD WOMAN

Especially the big ones.

The Old Woman's rasping laugh echoes through the dingy gloom.

CUT TO:

EXT. BORO PARK – NIGHT

The moon glows in the night sky. Tilt down to reveal:

The Horowitz's apartment building in Boro Park. There is a single window lit.

INT. HOROWITZ APARTMENT – NIGHT

Mendel is sitting at the table in the living-room studying a tractate of Talmud. He rubs his exhausted eyes, then gives in to his fatigue and closes the book.

INT. BATHROOM – NIGHT

Mendel bends over the sink, splashing his face with cold water.

INT. BEDROOM – NIGHT

Mendel stands in the middle of the room, dressed in his oversized pajamas. He takes in his solitude. He walks to his bed and sits down on it. He closes his eyes and moves his lips in a silent prayer. Then he switches off the bedside lamp and lies back. A moment of stillness . . .

Then Mendel jerks upright and switches the light back on. He hops out of bed, runs to the closet, throws open the door, yanks out his pants and begins pulling them on.

    CUT TO:

INT. ABANDONED BUILDING – NIGHT

CLOSE ON: *the rusted can, as the flame within it flickers out and dies. Rack focus to Sonia's face. Her eyes flutter open.*

The Old Woman is gone. A black shadow falls across the floor where she sat.

SONIA

Bubby?

The shadow glides across the floor, and Sonia's POV follows it as it moves to the doorway, where the figure casting it turns and disappears into the dark . . . the sound of footsteps descending creaky stairs.

Sonia stands up, rubbing her aching neck, and starts toward the doorway . . . then she hears the sound of the door opening downstairs, so instead she hurries to the paneless window and looks out.

Sonia's POV of the street. The figure exits the abandoned building and steps into the light . . . It's Yossi.

CLOSE ON: *Sonia, her eyes widening with disbelief. Yossi looks up at Sonia and smiles. Then he turns and starts walking away up the dark street.*

    CUT TO:

Schmuel, bleary eyed, in his pajamas, moves aside as Mendel steps through the doorway.

MENDEL

Where's Shimmie?

SCHMUEL

Shimmie? It's three a.m., Mendel. He's sleeping in the kids' room.

Mendel strides into the house, stopping outside the door to the kids' room – where Rachel, in her nightgown, is standing.

RACHEL

Mendel? Are you all right?

Mendel just nods and walks into the kids' room. Rachel and Schmuel exchange confused looks; then Mendel re-emerges, holding his now crying baby in his arms.

What are you doing, Mendel?

MENDEL

I'm taking my son home.

Rachel reaches for her brother's arm.

RACHEL

Mendel . . . listen to me – I understand how this must feel to you, but it's for the . . .

MENDEL

No, you listen to me. Shimmie is my son, and from now on, he sleeps by me. I'll be grateful for your help during the days, when I'm teaching – but from this moment on, every night I'll be doing my own learning at home, instead of the *besmedresh*. And when I'm home, my son's going to be by me.

RACHEL

This isn't just a matter of what you want, Mendel. Shimmie needs to be in . . .

That's *enough*, Rachel.

Rachel shuts up. Schmuel turns to Mendel . . . his voice is thick with emotion:

I'll get together a couple of the guys from the *besmedresh* who'll be happy to come over nights and learn at your house. We'll learn by you.

Mendel holds his son tightly. He nods gratefully at his brother-in-law.

CUT TO:

EXT. BUSHWICK, BROOKLYN. ELEVATED TRAIN STATION – NIGHT

The station doors fly open and Sonia steps out on to the platform at the top of the stairway. She stops and looks around frantically.

Sonia's POV of the street below. Yossi's slim figure passes through the pool of light under a street-lamp, then rounds the corner . . .

Whip pan back to:

Sonia – who immediately begins running down the stairs to the sidewalk.

EXT. BUSHWICK STREET – NIGHT

Sonia races around the corner, running as fast as her legs can carry her.

Sonia's POV of Yossi, walking casually, but somehow still far ahead of her. He is momentarily lit by a street-lamp and then he is swallowed up by the darkness beyond.

CUT TO:

Black.

The sound of a door being pounded. It swings open, revealing:

Ramon standing shirtless in the doorway. His eyes are red, jolted by adrenaline.

Sonia is standing out on the stoop, trembling and out of breath.

RAMON

Jesus.

He reaches out for her, and pulls her inside.

MATCH CUT TO:

INT. RAMON'S STUDIO – NIGHT

As Ramon guides Sonia into the frame, steadying her with his hands on her shoulders.

RAMON

Take it easy . . . it's gonna be all right.

SONIA

No it's not . . . nothing's going to be right ever again . . .

RAMON

Easy, Sonia . . . easy.

Ramon steps away from her and turns on a light, illuminating the dark studio.

Sonia shields her face.

SONIA

Don't.

Ramon stops. He turns and dims the light.

RAMON

You want something to drink? A glass of water or something? How about a beer?

SONIA

I just need somewhere . . . safe . . . to stay. Just for tonight.

RAMON

You can stay here.

Sonia nods, relieved, and sits down on a wooden box by Ramon's worktable.

SONIA

Thank you.

Ramon moves toward Sonia.

RAMON

Want to talk?

Sonia stays silent. Ramon kneels beside her and she averts her head.

SONIA

Please don't look at me.

Ramon draws back slightly. There is a moment of silence.

I'm so sorry to wake you up like this.

RAMON

I wasn't sleeping.

He stands up and steps over to his worktable.

After you took off down that street, the way you were talking,
I thought I was never gonna see you again. I cleaned off my
table and I ain't stopped working since. The whole time I've
been thinking about the way you walked, with your back held
up all straight, like you were cracking, but you wouldn't
break . . .

*Ramon lifts a cloth on which several pieces of jewelry are laid and holds
it in front of Sonia. Her eyes fill with tears.*

SONIA

They're . . . so beautiful. I don't even have the words . . .

RAMON

All my life I been trying to make up for my old man splitting
by lookin' out for my Moms – I don't mind, but it ain't
fuckin' easy. Then you walk in and I think, here's another
desperate woman who needs something from me. Freaked me
out. But I was wrong . . . I'm the one who needs you.

Sonia takes the cloth, folding it gently over the glittering pieces.

SONIA

No. You were right to be afraid of me. You need to create
and all I've ever done is destroy. I've destroyed myself and
I've destroyed every good thing I've ever known – but I won't
destroy you.

113

Sometimes a thing's got to be destroyed, you know? Walls got to be broke down so's you can find what they been hiding inside, all along.

Sonia looks at Ramon tenderly, in agony.

SONIA

Break down these walls and what you'll see is even more ugly than you could bear to look at.

Ramon looks long and hard at Sonia . . . then he bursts into a loud laugh.

Don't laugh at me.

Ramon starts to say something else – but stops himself. Instead he walks around the table to where his sculpture in progress – the man and woman intertwined – is standing on a pedestal in front of a 3-sided mirror so that it is visible from every angle. Ramon puts both hands against the sculpture, gives it a terrific shove and it crashes to the floor, shattering to pieces.

Sonia looks on in shock, as Ramon walks back to her, then gently steers her toward the 3-sided mirror.

RAMON

You can't even see yourself, can you?

He sits her down on the pedestal. Then he reaches up and touches the earring hanging from her ear.

This is nice, right? I agree. But that's all it is. It's a *chachka*. A nice little *chachka*.

He takes out the earring. Then he removes the kerchief covering Sonia's hair. It's the first time – other than the scene in the ritual bath – that Sonia's short, dark hair has been exposed. She flinches, reaching up nervously . . . but Ramon is already removing the other earring from her earlobe. He touches her cheek with his fingertips and turns her head slightly.

Three angles of Sonia's face look back at her from the mirrors.

He reaches around her neck, unfastening the necklace she is wearing.

This is a chain, Sonia. It's just a fucking chain.

He gently unbuttons the top few buttons of Sonia's blouse, exposing her throat and upper chest. He lifts her hand up, and gently slides the bracelet off her wrist.

Now look at you . . .

CLOSE ON: *Sonia's face – looking straight into the mirrors, as Ramon enters the frame in profile and whispers:*

You're beautiful.

Sonia turns slowly and looks at Ramon. Slowly, tentatively, their lips meet in a kiss.

FADE TO BLACK

A vertical silhouette, at first just a blur, slowly emerges from the darkness . . . coming into focus as:

Yossi, standing in front of a window, through which sunlight is streaming . . . He is naked, save for his underwear, and his hair is wet. He steps forward and stops at the edge of a bed.

YOSSI

Sonia?

Little Sonia, aged 8, looks at her brother with dreamy eyes.

SONIA

Yossi.

Yossi kneels in front of her.

YOSSI

I swam.

Little Sonia smiles.

SONIA

Me too.

Yossi reaches his hand out, and little Sonia takes it, her fingers closing over his.

CUT TO:

The adult Sonia's eyes flutter open. Her head is nestled in a white pillow, a shaft of sunlight illuminating her face . . . we follow her gaze:

Sonia's pale hand is intertwined with Ramon's dark one.

Ramon is lying curled up on the bed beside her, fast asleep.

A slight smile creeps into Sonia's eyes. She reaches with her free hand to touch his face but stops herself. She gently extracts her hand from his and slides herself to a sitting position at the edge of the bed . . .

Sonia's POV – of a statuette of the Virgin Mary on the tabletop by the wall. Mary's head is covered by a veil of mourning . . .

Sonia is gripped by emotion . . . then her face hardens with resolve, as she clearly understands what she has to do.

CUT TO:

EXT. THE REBBE'S HOUSE – DAY

The door opens, and the bearded face of the deceased Rebbe's Chief Gabbai peeks outside.

GABBAI

Yes?

REVERSE ON: *Sonia. She's not wearing a wig, or a kerchief and her blouse is open several buttons. Nothing radical, but she does not look like a young Hassidic girl anymore.*

SONIA

Is the Rebbitzn home?

GABBAI

What can I do for you?

SONIA

I'd like to speak to the Rebbitzn.

GABBAI

The Rebbitzn is still in mourning. She doesn't grant audience to strangers.

SONIA

My name is Sonia. Please tell the Rebbitzn that I am respectfully requesting a moment of her time.

GABBAI

I'm sorry, but like I said, the Rebbitzn won't . . .

Then there is a voice from within the house. The gabbai turns and listens for a moment, then looks back at Sonia. He indicates her neckline.

Make yourself decent before you come in.

SONIA

If you don't like the way I look, look at your shoes or stick your nose in a book. It's your problem, not mine.

She brushes past him and enters the house.

INT. REBBE'S HOUSE. LIVING-ROOM – DAY

Sonia steps inside, tailed by the gabbai. The old Rebbitzn is standing in the middle of the room, a vision in black.

GABBAI

I'm sorry, Rebbitzn, but this woman wouldn't listen to . . .

REBBITZN

Yaakov.

The gabbai stops talking. The Rebbitzn motions with her hand. The gabbai casts a last, resentful glance at Sonia, then turns on his heel and exits.

WIDE ON: *the room, as the two women regard each other in silence. Then:*

SONIA

At the eulogy for the Rebbe, may his memory be a blessing, you came to me. You whispered in my ear. You said:

CUT TO:

EXT. REBBE FUNERAL – DAY

QUICK CUT: *Sonia and the Rebbitzn, surrounded by mourners. The Rebbitzn leans over and puts her lips near Sonia's ear . . .*

SONIA'S VOICE
(*off-screen*)

Thank you.

CUT TO:

BACK TO: *Sonia – in the present. She looks into the Rebbitzn's eyes . . .*

SONIA

Why?

The Rebbitzn waits for a moment . . . then she speaks softly:

REBBITZN

I was here, on the day you spoke to Moishe. Your words rekindled a fire in a body that was too old to contain it and, like a flash, he was consumed.
(*pauses, remembering*)
His eyes were looking into mine – and the last words to pass

his lips before he left this world were: 'I love you.' It was the first time in twenty years he spoke those words to me.

Sonia's eyes are wide, awestruck.

You took a man away from his people forever. But for one night you gave a wife back her husband. He left his people, so they wept. But he found me . . . So I thanked you.
(pauses)
Perhaps I sound selfish to you. But you are still young, and I am very old. Some day, you might understand me.

SONIA

I understand you. But with all due respect – I don't plan on waiting for some day.

The Rebbitzn slowly nods.

I don't belong here, Rebbitzn. I know that now . . . and I've paid a heavy price for it. I'm leaving my child here. It's like a knife in my heart – but until I know where I do belong, I'm sure it's for the best.

Her voice hardens with determination.

There is still something here that belongs to me, however. I accept your gratitude . . . for returning to you what should have always been yours. Now I'm asking you to help me reclaim what is mine.

CUT TO:

EXT. BORO PARK STREET – DAY

Long lens looking down the block – as Sonia strides purposefully up the sidewalk, flanked on either side by young Hassidic men, a half-dozen in all. Their black fedoras are tilted, their tzitzis flying; they look like a bunch of cowboys . . .

REVERSE ANGLE: *as the 'Wild Bunch' walk past the camera heading down the street toward the front stoop of Sender's store.*

Nelson looks on in confusion, stepping in the way of the door. Then he instinctively moves out of the way as Sonia and the phalanx of Hassidim march past him and into the building.

INT. BASEMENT 'STORE' – DAY

The door flies open, and one of the young Hassidim steps inside, followed by Sonia and the others.

The Two Men sitting at the desk where Sonia used to do business look up in shock. One, Engleberg, is a thin, bearded Hassid who is Sender's new salesman. The other is Mr Fishbein, Sonia's overly admiring middle-aged client.

> ENGLEBERG
> What's the meaning of this?

> SONIA
> You're Sender's new guy?

Engleberg looks at Sonia . . . then at the half-dozen Hassidim behind her. He nods.

Mr Fishbein has finally recognized Sonia. He stands up wearing an incredulous grin.

Mrs Horowitz? My God, you look absolutely fantastic, if I may say so my −

SONIA

Sit down, Mr Fishbein. I'm not in the mood.

Then there is the sound of a creaking door . . . all heads turn:

Sender has entered the room through the door leading upstairs. He stands there, holding a sheaf of invoices in his meaty hand. He looks at the gang of gabbaim, then fixes his gaze on Sonia.

Sonia meets Sender's eyes with her own steely glare . . . then she turns to Engleberg.

I assume the combination to the safe has been changed since I left. Please be so good as to open it. There is an item in there that belongs to me. These men were all gabbaim to the Rebbe, and are of unassailable character. They will be witnesses to the fact that I will take only that which is my property and nothing else.

ENGLEBERG
(*nervous laugh*)

This is a joke.

SONIA

If you don't open that safe, Mr New Guy, I promise you it's gonna end with a very ugly punchline.

Engleberg looks at the Hassidim.

The Chief Gabbai nods.

Engleberg turns helplessly to Sender.

Sender looks at Sonia for a moment . . . Then he steps over to the wall safe. He turns the dial several times and the lock clicks open. Sender puts the invoices down on the desk, buttons up his jacket and walks toward the exit . . . and stops as Sonia steps into his way. She whispers:

Now I'm free.

A slight smile creeps into Sender's eyes. Then he starts forward again, and the young gabbaim part to the sides of the doorway as Sender passes through and leaves the room.

CUT TO:

The gold ring rising into the frame – completely filling the screen. Then we rack focus to:

Ramon's green eyes – taking it in . . . then looking beyond it:

Sonia is standing in front of him, holding the ring.

SONIA

I couldn't bear the thought of your muse going empty-handed – when you find her.

She hands the ring to Ramon. They are standing in his studio, very close to each other.

I hope she'll be as inspiring to you as you've been to me.

Ramon takes Sonia's hand, and raises it.

RAMON

She already has been.

He starts to slide the ring on to Sonia's finger, but she stops him, closing his own hand around it again.

RAMON

It's yours.

SONIA

I'm gonna ask you to hold on to it for me for a little while, okay?

Sonia turns, and walks toward the door.

RAMON

Sonia . . .

(*she stops*)

Where you going?

Sonia thinks it over for a moment, then she smiles:

                              SONIA
          I don't know.

                              RAMON
          If you need a place to . . . I mean . . .

Ramon walks over to Sonia.

          Stay with me.

They look into one another's eyes . . . then:

                              VOICE
                           (*off-screen*)
          Ramon . . . *Hay un varon procurando a la juvenita.*

*Ramon's mother is standing in the doorway leading upstairs. Ramon
turns to Sonia.*

                              RAMON
          There's someone upstairs who wants to see you.

                           MRS GARCIA
          El dice ser su esposo.

Ramon takes that in, then looks closely at Sonia:

                              RAMON
          He says he's your husband.

Sonia can't believe her ears. She steadies herself.

                              SONIA
          I should talk to him.

Ramon nods.

                              RAMON
          You got a life – go do what you got to do.
                           (*smiles*)
          I'm not going anywhere.

INT. GARCIA HOME. LIVING-ROOM – DAY

WIDE ON: *the room – Mendel is waiting there. His back is toward us,
hands clasped behind him. He rocks nervously on his heels, looking at*

                              124

the overwhelming display of Christian paraphernalia spread out before him. If ever the phrase 'fish out of water' applied, this is it.

Sonia quietly enters the frame in the foreground.

Mendel looks over his shoulder. He sees her and turns around.

> SONIA
>
> Mendel.

> MENDEL
>
> Sonia. You look . . . nice.

> SONIA
>
> You too.

> MENDEL
>
> Sender told me where I could find you . . . in case you were wondering.

> SONIA
>
> I wasn't.

Mendel ducks his head sheepishly.

> SONIA
>
> How's Shimmie?

> MENDEL
>
> Good. He stays by me, now.

> SONIA
>
> That's good.

> MENDEL
>
> I'm sure he misses you.

> SONIA
>
> And you?

Mendel looks up.

> Do you miss me?

Mendel hesitates, uncomfortable, then gently shakes his head.

MENDEL

You?

Sonia smiles a rueful smile, then shakes her head as well, and both of them break into laughter.

Mendel composes himself, the sadness creeping back into his face.

I just came by because I wanted to tell you . . .

He steps forward, and crosses the room until he's in front of Sonia.

. . . I'm sorry I forgot your birthday.

Sonia can't believe it. She looks at Mendel with incredulous eyes.

SONIA

My birthday? Do you think . . . that's what this was all about?

Mendel looks up at his wife. His eyes are sad, and wise.

MENDEL

Of course not. I've been doing a lot of thinking, about things that I never understood how to think about before. I know that the pain we caused each other couldn't be helped – I am who I am, and you are who you are, and we just weren't meant to be together. There was nothing either of us could have done other than what we did.
(*pauses*)
But I was wrong to have forgotten your birthday.

Mendel reaches into his pocket and takes out a small black box.

SONIA

Mendel . . . Mendel, you know I can't accept a . . .

MENDEL

Please take it. If not for yourself, then for me. Yom Kippur's coming up, and I want to face God knowing I tried to do right by you.

Sonia takes the box. She opens it:

A single ruby is nestled in a bed of black velvet.

SONIA

A ruby . . .

MENDEL

Your birthstone. I looked it up.

Sonia turns it in the light.

SONIA

It's flawless.

MENDEL

I bought it loose. I figured finding the right setting for it is your speciality, so why interfere?

Sonia looks at Mendel, her eyes glittering.

Please come by and visit – evenings, shabbes, whenever you can. Shimmie should know he has a mother who loves him.

SONIA

And . . . the others? What will they say?

MENDEL

What others? As far as Shimmie is concerned, the only voices that matter belong to his mother and father.

Sonia is unable to speak. Mendel reaches over, and gently takes her face in his hands . . . their faces are close, as if their lips might touch . . . but instead Mendel gently plants a kiss on Sonia's forehead, and steps away.

Mendel walks to the door and opens it.

SONIA
(*off-screen*)

Mendel . . .

Mendel looks back at Sonia.

God bless you.

Mendel smiles. Then he turns and steps outside.

CLOSE ON: *Sonia. Her expression a mixture of sorrow and happiness, as the light from the open doorway brightly illuminates her face.*

CUT TO BLACK

END CREDITS SEQUENCE

Over the credits, in extreme close-up, Ramon's skillful fingers fit the ruby into the empty setting of the golden ring until it is a perfect whole. On the image of the finished ring . . .

FADE OUT

CREDITS

SONIA	Renée Zellweger
SENDER	Christopher Eccleston
RACHEL	Julianna Margulies
RAMON	Allen Payne
MENDEL	Glenn Fitzgerald
REBBITZN	Kim Hunter
REBBE	John Randolph
BEGGAR WOMAN	Kathleen Chalfant
SCHMUEL	Peter Jacobson
FEIGA	Edie Falco
DR BAUER	Tim Jerome
MRS GELBART	Phyllis Newman
SHAINDY	Joyce Reehling
YOSSI	Shelton Dane
YOUNG SONIA	Jackie Ryan
HRUNDI KAPOOR	Faran Tahir
MR BERMAN	Martin Shakar
MRS GARCIA	Teodorina Bello
CHIEF GABBAI	Glenn Fleshler
YOUNG GABBAI #1	Adam Dannheisser
GABBAI #2	Stephen Singer
GABBAI #3	Marvin Einhorn
DOCTOR	Mark Zimmerman
THE MOEL	Richard 'Izzy' Lifschutz
BARUCH	David Deblinger
HESHIE	Sam Jennings
TSIPI	Erin Rakow
YECHIEL	Asher Tabak
MR FISHBEIN	Allen Swift
NELSON	Daryl Edwards
MR SUGARMAN	Peter Slutsker
SONIA'S MOTHER	Lauren Klein
EARRING WOMAN	Tonye Patano
TY	Don Wallace
HOMEGIRL	Asia Minor
HOMEGIRL #2	Rosanna Plasencia
MR ENGELBERG	Jerry Matz

YOUNG HASSID	Michael Stuhlbarg
YOUNG WOMAN	Karen Contreras
LADY VENDOR	Wai Ching Ho
PARANOID VENDOR	Mel Duane Gionson
SMOOTH VENDOR	Paul J. O. Lee
ISRAEL WOMAN	Leyla Aalam

CREW

Written and Directed by	Boaz Yakin
Produced by	Lawrence Bender
	John Penotti
Executive Producers	Bob Weinstein
	Harvey Weinstein
Co-Producer	Joann Fregalette Jansen
Line Producer	Adam Brightman
Director of Photography	Adam Holender A.S.C.
Production Designer	Dan Leigh
Editor	Arthur Coburn A.C.E.
Costume Designer	Ellen Lutter
Music by	Lesley Barber
Post Production Supervisor	Heidi Vogel
Title Sequence Designed and Produced by	Dan Perri
First Assistant Director	David Wechsler
Second Assistant Director	Marco Londoner
Second Second Assistant Director	Rick Lange
Assistant Editor-LA	Blacke Maniquis
Assistant Editor-NY	Anne McCabe
Second Assistant Editor	Gregg Apirian
Camera Operator	Chris Hayes
First Assistant Camera	John Cambria
Second Assistant Camera	Michael Cambria
Camera Trainee	Francis A. Porter
Steadicam Operator	Andrew Casey
Still Photographer	Abbot Genser
Script Supervisor	Mary Gambardella
Dialect Consultant	Jess Platt
Sound Mixer	William Sarokin
Boom Operator	George Leong
Second Boom	Richard Murphy
Key Grip	William A. Miller

Best Boy Grip	Michael Betzag
Dolly Grip	John Donohue
Company Grips	Nicky 'Nuckles' Vaccaro
	Christopher Vaccaro
	Joseph Donohue III
	Damien F. Donohue
Key Rigging Grip	Craig Vaccaro
Gaffer	Scott Ramsey
Best Boy Electric	Mark Schwenter
Electric	Rocco Palmieri
	Michael McDonald
	Michael Reed
	Linda Philipps
	Shaun C. Gilbert
Shop Electric	John Billeci
Wardrobe Supervisors	Winsome G. McKoy
	Barbara Krauthamer
Costume Shopper	Sally Lesser
Assistant to Ellen Lutter	Denise T. Davidson
Key Makeup Artist	Lori Hicks
Key Hairstylists	John D. Quaglia
	Wayne Herndon
Set Decorator	Leslie E. Rollins
Leadman	Christopher J. Detita
Set Dressers	Mitch Towse
	John J. Flugel
	Dennis Lee Causey
On Set Dresser	Robert Currie
Draftperson	William Stabile
Art Department Facilitator	Eryka Seimon Henderson
Production Assistant	Corey Bobker
Special Effects Coordinator	John M. Ottesen
Property Master	Kevin C. Ladson
Assistant Property Master	Tyler H. Kim
Construction Coordinator	Brent Haywood
Foreman	Kenneth Stopsky
Standby Carpenter	Duncan Hoxworth
Carpenters	Ulf Loven
	James J. Curry
	Salvatore Sirico

	Rodney Clark
Construction Key Grip	Peter Anthony Betulia
Construction Grip	Robert A. Conroy
Charge Scenic Artist	Ann Haywood
Camera Scenic Artist	Rossana Fiore
Scenic Artists	Laura G. Gillen
	Julius Kozlowski
	Cyd Fenwick
	Elizabeth Goodall
	Gary Wimmer
Sculptures by	Elaine Houseman
Location Manager	Seth Burch
Assistant Location Manager	Joseph Zolfo
Assistant Location Manager	Gary Scott
Stage Manager	Jeremy D. Pratt
Location Assistants	Alexander Berberich
	Janet Henry
	Jabbar E. McDonald
Location Scout	Tom Betterton
Parking Coordinator	Kerry Clark
Parking Production Assistant	Yogi
Craft Service	Joe Facey
Production Coordinator	Ellen Gannon
Production Associate	Anita Sum
Production Secretary	Andrew Vogliano
Production Assistant	Alicia Haldenwang
Production Accountant	Margo A. Myers
Assistant Accountant	Marlus C. Harding
Payroll Accountant	John B. Finn
Post Production Coordinator	Tracey D'Arcy
Post Production Accountants	Owen & Desalvo Co.
	Deborah Owen
	Henry Winston
	Jason Cramer
Supervising Sound Editor	Robert Fitzgerald
Sound Effects Editors	Robert Fitzgerald
	Elizabeth Flaum
Dialog Editors	Paul Curtis
	Frederick H. Stahly
	Stuv
Assistant Sound Editor	Tim Rakoczy
Dialog Assistant	Pembrooke Andrews

	Sean Kennelly
ADR Mixer	Jeff Vaughn, C.A.S.
ADR Recordist	Jason Lezama
ADR Editors	Stuv
	Frederick H. Stahly
Foley Mixer	Eric Thompson, C.A.S.
Foley Artists	Joan Rowe
	Sean Rowe
	Katie Rowe
	Alan Kerr
Foley Editors	Jason Lezama
	John Chandler
Music Editor	Dan Diprima
Digital Sound Services by	EFX Systems, Burbanks, CA
Digital Rerecording by	Creative Cafe, Los Angeles
Rerecording Mixers	Sergio Reyes
	B. Tennyson Sebastian III
Music Contractor	David Low
Music Conducted by	Ken Kugler
Music Engineered by	Stuart Brawley
Music Copyist	Jo Ann Kane Music Service
Negative Cutter	Gary Burritt
Color Timer	Phil Hetos
Titles by	Cinema Research Corporation
Opticals	Balsmeyer & Everett, Inc.
	Pacific Title
Key Set Production Assistant	Neil Orlowski
Set Production Assistants	James E. Sheridan
	Kali Rashad Harrison
	Peter Dominick
	Hunter Carson
	Jay Richard Piro
Assistants to Lawrence Bender	Courtney McDonnell
	Jeff Swafford
Assistant to John Penotti	Jennifer Yun
Transportation Captain	John Leonidas
Co-Captain	Dennis Radesky
Driver-Electric	Robert Lansing
Driver-Grip	Richard Battista
Drivers-Prop	William Baker
Driver-Camera	Robert Dwyer
Driver-Set Dressing	Barry Sweeney

133

Driver-Hair/MU-Wardrobe	Luis Rodriguez
Driver-Swing	Kevin P. Griffin
Driver-Maxi Van	Ronald Dennis Drogan
Driver-Honeywagon	Leo Fotopoulos
Unit Publicist	Tom Piechura
Casting Associates	Jordan Beswick
	Dena Trakes
Product Placement	Ruthie Tanami
Caterer-Stage	Something's Cooking
Caterer-Location	Antonucci Catering
Clearances	Marshall & Plumb
Completion Bond	Film Finances
	Kurt Woolner
	Maureen Duffy
Camera	Panavision New York
Film	Eastman Kodak
Insurance	Great Northern/Reiff & Associates
Payroll	Axium Entertainment Services
Dailies Processed by	Duart Film Laboratoires, Inc
Production Sound Transfer by	Magno Sound & Video
Color by	Deluxe
Legal	Lighter, Crossman
	Nichols & Adler, Inc
	Carlos Goodman
	Jeff Springer
	Ann Du Val
Ramon's Studio Consultant	Robin David Ludwig
	The Hammer
Group ADR Coordinator	Burton Sharp
Loop Group	Jerome Best
	Jake Chipps
	Joyce Goldman
	Henry Goldscher
	Eddie Herschler
	Bernard Hiller
	Winnie Hiller
	Lev Mailer
	Sally Rainer
	Burton Sharp
	Bill Stern
	Glen-Bob Sweet
	Shane Sweet

'AROVECHA'
Performed by
JESUS ALEMANYS ICUBANISMOI
Written by ORLANDO VALLE
Courtesy of Hannibal Records,
A RYODIC LABEL
By Arrangement with
OCEAN PARK MUSIC GROUP

'YO SIEMPRE ODDARA'
Performed by JANE BUNNETT
(From the CD 'Spirits of Havana')
Written by GUILLERMO BARETTO
& JANE BUNNETT
Courtesy of JANE BUNNETT
& CANADIAN BROADCASTING CORP.